"*Brooklyn Goes Home* is about human love and compassion on the one hand and callousness and cruelty on the other. It's also the incredible account of how two brave and committed people successfully fought against a shameless, yet powerful, industry. Christine and Carey had little more than a belief in themselves and a shared love for their greyhound Brooklyn, but their determination has paid off for thousands of other dogs in the United States and worldwide. My greyhound and I recommend you read this stunning memoir!"

—**Dr. Jane Goodall**, PhD, DBE; Founder of the Jane Goodall Institute and UN Messenger of Peace

"This book is a must-read for activists—full of gripping stories and inspiring lessons. Christine and Carey overcame personal challenges, built a movement, and got a big win for animals. They walk and talk you through how to fight for animals against powerful—and scary—exploiters. Read this book and see how a few motivated people organized and abolished a cruel entertainment."

—**Jim Mason**; Attorney, author of *An Unnatural Order*, and co-author of *The Ethics of What we Eat and Animal Factories*

"If you think you cannot make a difference because you have little or no resources and face wealthy, powerful opposition, read this book. You will be inspired. This story is a testimony to the ability of intense passion, unwavering determination, and unrelenting persistence to prevail over money and power when fighting for a just cause."

—**Carole Baskin**; CEO of Big Cat Rescue

"Every greyhound is an individual. Each has their personality and wants and needs, fears and desires. The lucky ones are rescued, becoming beloved family members, acting as ambassadors for their kind in need of our help. Christine A. Dorchak and Carey M. Theil, founders of the US-based, anti-greyhound racing non-profit organisation GREY2K USA Worldwide, tell the must-read story of one ambassador, Brooklyn. In *Brooklyn Goes Home*, Dorchak and Theil write about their successful international campaigns to educate the public and persuade elected representatives to end the greyhound racing industry. They also describe Brooklyn's moving story as a rescued greyhound from her birth on a puppy farm in Australia, forced to race in China, and eventually, freedom living in their home in the USA."

—**Kim Stallwood**; Animal Rights Author and
Independent Scholar

"If you love dogs, and rare is the human who does not, you will want to read this amazing chronicle describing the successful fight to free greyhounds from the cruelty of commercial racing. Do yourself a favor and read this book!"

—**Jeffrey Moussaieff Masson**; Author of *When Elephants Weep*
and Dogs Never Lie About Love

"*Brooklyn Goes Home* is the heartwarming and inspirational memoir of Christine Dorchak and Carey Theil, two of the smartest and most dedicated animal advocates I have ever known. Over the last twenty years, they have worked from the ground up to close down dozens of dog tracks state by state, and now worldwide. If you want an inside look into the politics and strategy of successful grassroots campaigning, this is the book for you."

—**Chris DeRose**; President and Founder of Last Chance for
Animals, Author of *In Your Face: From Actor to Animal Activist*

"If you ever had any doubt that greyhound racing never should have begun, no less continued to grow as a highly abusive and heartless global bloodsport, please read this outstanding book. Brooklyn's story, along with that of his loving humans, will move you deeply and must be shared worldwide. This outstanding book is a model for what needs to be done to end all sorts of horrific animal abuse."

—**Marc Bekoff**, Ph.D.; Author of *The Emotional Lives of Animals*, *The Animals' Agenda*, and *Demystifying Dogs: An A-to-Z Guide to All Things Canine*

"Human history is built upon ordinary people doing extraordinary things, a truth we are reminded of once again in this awe-inspiring and entertaining story of the international movement to abolish greyhound racing. There was never a grassroots movement for predatory gambling on greyhounds. Instead, it was driven by the greed of commercialized gambling operators and a lust for power by some public officials from both political parties. But this book is a testimony there is unquestionably an impassioned and vibrant grassroots movement to end the cruel practice. Brooklyn's story, coupled with the work of Christine, Carey, and their colleagues, is one that will inevitably inspire you to act to do the work and endure the sacrifices it takes to help make the world a more just, merciful, and forgiving place."

—**Les Bernal**; National Director of Stop Predatory Gambling

Brooklyn Goes Home

*The Rise and Fall of American Greyhound Racing
and the Dog that Inspired a Movement*

Christine A. Dorchak and Carey M. Theil

Lantern Publishing & Media • Woodstock & Brooklyn, NY

2023
Lantern Publishing & Media
PO Box 1350
Woodstock, NY 12498
www.lanternpm.org

Cover design by Emily Lavieri-Scull
Copyediting and typesetting by Pauline Lafosse

Printed in the United States of America

Library of Congress Cataloging-in-Publication Data

Names: Dorchak, Christine A., 1966- author. | Theil, Carey M., 1978- author.
Title: Brooklyn goes home : the rise and fall of American greyhound racing, and the dog that inspired a movement / by Christine A. Dorchak, and Carey M. Theil.
Other titles: Rise and fall of American greyhound racing, and the dog that inspired a movement
Description: Woodstock : Lantern Publishing & Media, 2024.
Identifiers: LCCN 2023008423 (print) | LCCN 2023008424 (ebook) | ISBN 9781590567142 (paperback) | ISBN 9781590567159 (epub)
Subjects: LCSH: Greyhound racing—United States—History. | Greyhounds—United States. | Dog rescue—United States. | Dog rescue. | Human-animal relationships—United States. | GREY2K USA (Organization) | Brooklyn (Greyhound), 2008-2022. | BISAC: NATURE / Animal Rights | SPORTS & RECREATION / Animal Sports / Dog Racing
Classification: LCC SF440 .D67 2024 (print) | LCC SF440 (ebook) | DDC 798.8/50973—dc23/eng/20230627
LC record available at https://lccn.loc.gov/2023008423
LC ebook record available at https://lccn.loc.gov/2023008424

Contents

ACKNOWLEDGEMENTS

It would be impossible to thank everyone who made this book possible. First and foremost, we are grateful to everyone who has fought for the greyhounds. This is their story.

Our campaigns against dog racing would never have been conceived without our inspiring mothers, Lillian Dorchak and Connie Theil, and our honorary mother, Paula Blanchard. We have had the good fortune to surround ourselves with dedicated board members and staff over the years, including Reverend Tom Grey, Kevin Neuman, Dr. Jill Hopfenbeck, Eric Jackson, Sherry Mangold, Jay Kirkus, Charmaine Settle, Kathy Pelton, Joyce Carta, Caryn Wood, Denise McFadden, Amelia Cook, Patrick Baga, Emma Coppock, Kat Thomas, Jess Weller, Dana Demetrio, Caroline Williams, Maria Moyser, and Danielle Festa, whose enchanting portrait of Brooklyn appears on our cover.

To Jon Albano, Meaghan Kent, Marisa Alfonso and the entire firm of Morgan, Lewis & Bockius, we thank you for your expertise. We are forever grateful to the mentors and colleagues who paved the way for our efforts, including Dr. Peter Singer, Steve Wise, Jim Mason, Kim Stallwood, Wayne Pacelle, Judge Sarah Luick, Kara Holmquist, Susan Netboy, Paige Powell, Sara Amundson, Dennis Tabella, Albano Martins, Geoff Wyatt and Paul Littlefair, to name just a few. We also want to recognize David Vaughn, Daryl Elliott and Doug Rubin for inviting us to take the leap of faith that opened the door to the great adventure of the last twenty-five years. Without the longtime support of Eddie DeBartolo, Jr. of

Florida and Tom Scholz, founder of the band *Boston*, we would never have succeeded.

We especially wish to thank S. Matt Read and Avi Nelson, both of whom read early versions of our manuscript and helped us through a difficult process which left every page stained with tears.

Finally, we would like to thank our two greyhound angels Brooklyn and Gina. It is our sincere hope that they are together somewhere, on the far side of the rainbow, running free.

(Maria Moyser/GREY2K USA Worldwide)

FOREWORD

JANE GOODALL

I have always loved animals. From age ten, I dreamed of going to live with wild animals in Africa and writing books about them. I never thought of becoming a scientist, just a naturalist. Through hard work, a supportive mother—and luck—I got to study and learn from our closest living relatives, chimpanzees, with whom we share some 98.6% of the structure of our DNA. When I had been in the field for about a year my mentor, Louis Leakey insisted I earn a doctorate so that my results would be taken seriously by the scientific community. So in 1961 I arrived at Cambridge University to work for a PhD in ethology. (I didn't even know what ethology was and there was no internet back then!) Imagine how I felt when I was told, by eminent scientists, that I had done everything wrong. That the chimpanzees in my writings should have been numbered, not named, and that I could not talk about their personalities, minds or emotions—because these were qualities unique to humans. In other words humans were to hold ourselves apart from the rest of the animal kingdom. Fortunately I had a wonderful teacher when I was a child who taught me that in this respect my professors were completely wrong. That teacher was my dog, Rusty. You cannot share your life in a meaningful way with a dog, cat, horse, pig, bird—or any animal—and not come to KNOW that Homo sapiens are not the only beings on this planet with personalities, minds and emotions.

Rusty was not a greyhound (he was a delightful mutt), but it was thanks to him that I was able to stand firm against the reductionist attitude of science towards animals. Then gradually, especially when documentary films began showing chimpanzee behaviour in the wild, my unorthodox thinking became accepted. An article I once submitted to the prestigious journal *Nature* came back to me with the following comments: Every time I wrote 'he' or 'she' my personal pronouns were crossed out and replaced with 'it.' And 'who' was replaced with 'which.' Angrily I crossed out the 'its' and 'whichs'—and in the end my language was published! My first major victory. Today students are studying the intelligence of all animals—not only primates, elephants and whales, but pigs, rats, birds, octopuses . . . and of course, dogs.

My family has adopted two greyhounds, both of whom won a number of races before reaching their 'sell by' date. The first, Callie, was found by (one of the few) caring British breeders who had gone to Ireland to look for good dogs to enlarge the gene pool. He found her half-starved and tied to a tree in a layby. But he saw her potential, rescued her, built up her strength—and she repaid him by winning a number of races. When she broke her leg he had it fixed. Then, after she won several more races, he retired her to live with a friend of his. But after a short time the friend died, and that's when she came to live with us for the last four years of her life. The hound we have now, Khai, also won a number of her races. Fortunately, she was released to a rescue centre, where she remained until we were lucky enough to find her.

Our two greyhounds were individuals and quite different. Sandy-coated Callie was five years old when she joined us. She was gentle, very loving, and quite the opposite of intelligent. Jet black Khai was four years old when we rescued her. She was very shy and nervous for the first few months, but gradually her true personality emerged. She is *highly* intelligent, a real glutton, and an unashamed and cunning thief! She is mischievous and becoming more playful by the day. At certain times she goes crazy with the joys of life and runs "zoomies" around the room, throwing her toys in the air. And she spends hours sniffing around my garden.

Because all greyhounds do not find the salvation that Callie and Khai did, the fight to end dog racing is one of great importance. Even those greyhounds who are saved by groups like GREY2K USA Worldwide will spend their early days in terrible confinement, ever at risk of suffering broken legs, broken necks, paralysis, seizures (and more) every time they are let out of their cramped cages to race.

Brooklyn Goes Home is about human love and compassion on the one hand and callousness and cruelty on the other. It's also the incredible account of how two brave and committed people successfully fought against a shameless, yet powerful, industry. Their successes were (and are) hard won, and often came as a result of lessons learned from previous bitter failures—along with a determination to never give up. Christine and Carey had little more than a belief in themselves and a shared love for their greyhound Brooklyn, but their grit has paid off for thousands of other dogs in the United States and worldwide.

I hope that this book will encourage those fighting to end greyhound racing in all countries, and also serve to inspire those combatting other forms of seemingly-insurmountable animal abuse industries and practices. For its message is clear: no matter how disillusioned we feel when our efforts are defeated—we must never give up! We must go on fighting until the animals win.

For the animals,

—Dr. Jane Goodall, PhD, DBE
Founder of the Jane Goodall Institute
& UN Messenger of Peace

Prologue

The Prisoner

"The only sure bet is that within three years of arriving in Macau, every one of these greyhounds will be dead."
—South China Morning Post reporter Simon Parry

We once met a greyhound who changed the world. His name was Brooklyn. In telling his story, we could simply describe what it was like to live with this unique dog and how loving him changed our individual lives. But he was much more than just our family friend.

Mark Twain once said that truth is stranger than fiction, something which was more than apparent in our case! It's hard to imagine that a spotted dog would become the inspiration for a worldwide fight; that the campaign would be successful, and that after a decade of suffering, he would come home to us. And yet it happened. In fact, the thirteen short years that Brooklyn spent on this earth would turn out to be one of the most consequential periods in history for greyhounds, and for the broader debate on non-human animal rights. The life of this one dog signaled not only the end of dog racing in the United States, but also the emergence of the first movement to outlaw an animal abuse industry that was powerful, culturally resonant, and economically significant.

In truth, our work to end dog racing started years before we met him, but the fight to save his life sparked what is now a global movement. The pages ahead describe a circuitous series of events that led us to understand that change is possible. In fact, it is absolutely inevitable if we only believe in ourselves.

(Maria Moyser/GREY2K USA Worldwide)

Brooklyn was born on December 10, 2008. On that day, a red fawn greyhound named Miss Clementine had a litter of eleven puppies on a farm in New South Wales, Australia. Clementine had failed as a racer and was now producing her third litter, this time mated with a seven-year-old dog named Over Flo. A son of revered champion Brett Lee, Over Flo had initially shown promise on the track and won four of his initial races. When he fell and was injured in his tenth outing, his career as a runner was cut short.

Among Miss Clementine's and Over Flo's puppies was a small white and fawn boy who had brown spots like a Guernsey cow. They called him "Brooklyn." He was sent to the track the following year and raced a total of seven times at venues in Dapto, Bulli, and Goulburn. As an adult dog he was strong, with a broad frame and large, expressive brown eyes.

Like his mother, Brooklyn was a poor racer. He never finished above fifth place and earned a career total of only $140. This was a common fate for his littermates, and only his brother Desperate Dan made any real profit. Another brother, Earlwood Wonder, won a paltry sum of $50 in prize money. Two of Brooklyn's sisters disappeared from official records altogether, while one other was listed but never given a name.

By September 2010, at the tender age of twenty-one-months, Brooklyn's career as an Australian racing dog was over. Cast aside, his "owner" decided to make one final score on the young greyhound. He sold him off to race at the Yat Yuen Canidrome, the only legal dog track in China. Owned by Stanley Ho, a powerful billionaire linked to organized crime, the Canidrome was a bleak place. No greyhound ever got out alive because once a dog slowed down or aged out, he was killed and summarily replaced. Hundreds of unwanted Australian greyhounds were routinely shipped to the Canidrome to race, then die, each year.

Upon his arrival, Brooklyn was placed in a small, dark, and empty concrete cell, with no bed and no toys. He was a prisoner who had committed no crime. Sitting alone, Brooklyn must have endured profound loneliness and stress as weeks turned to months, and months became years. But unbeknownst to him, a small ray of hope had begun to appear beyond the horizon. Five weeks before he was even born and nearly ten thousand miles away, the citizens of Massachusetts decisively voted to outlaw commercial dog racing. Their votes, cast on a crisp November day, shuttered two historic and powerful racetracks and brought freedom to thousands of greyhounds. This was the beginning of the end of American dog racing, a struggle that would one day reach the shores of Macau. For the first time, Brooklyn had a chance to survive what was known as the "deadliest dog track in the world."

Brooklyn in his cage at the Canidrome in Macau
(Albano Martins/ANIMA Macau)

What follows is the story of the rise and fall of commercial greyhound racing in the United States and an account of how our small non-profit emerged from the ashes of a failed political campaign to make an impact. Finally, it is a remembrance of our three glorious years with a magical dog. We hope that readers will find inspiration in our chronicle, and perhaps discover new paths to making positive change in the world.

This history is based on the memories and reflections of Christine Dorchak and Carey Theil and describes twenty years of working together to help greyhounds. The two of us grew up more than a decade apart, on alternate coasts, one raised very traditionally and the other quite liberally, one an animal loving "Jersey Girl" turned lawyer, the other a poet and chess master turned political strategist. This Yin and Yang turned out to be a curious balance of opposites that is perhaps the reason that our organization survived and even succeeded against very great odds.

Even beyond our own odd couple status, what follows is a tale of strange bedfellows and unusual heroes. We hope to introduce you to the many wonderful people who joined us year after year, often from clashing sides, to become like-minded champions for the greyhounds. We will describe these people and our journey through the life of Brooklyn. For the ease of the reader, parts of our story are written in third person, but this memoir is entirely our own.

CHAPTER 1

THE BLOOMERS

"Finally, one gentleman came into my office, and asked, 'You know what your name is worth today?' I replied, 'I don't know what you mean.' He said, 'It is worth $100,000 on this racing bill.' I answered, "Well, if it's worth that much I believe I'll keep it.'"

—Florida Governor Doyle E. Carlton

Greyhound racing was born as an illegal enterprise, a form of gambling promoted by organized crime figures at the start of the twentieth century. The first recognized commercial greyhound racetrack in the USA was built in Emeryville, California, in 1919 by Owen Patrick Smith and the Blue Star Amusement Company. The track was oval in design and featured Smith's new invention, the mechanical lure, thought to offer a more humane alternative to the live lures used in traditional greyhound field coursing. By 1930, sixty-seven dog tracks had opened across the country—none of them legal.

The first of the new tracks placed Smith's lure running on the outside rail, while some other tracks used the inside rail. Dogs at Smith's tracks wore colored collars for identification, while dogs at other tracks wore racing blankets that would eventually become the industry standard. Initially, two-dog races were common; the number of dogs was later increased to as many as eight. Some dogs had to run several times in one afternoon to fill the day's schedule, known as the "racing card."

Despite duplicitous schemes to hide betting, such as the purchase of "options" or "shares" on winning dogs, tracks were regularly exposed as venues for illegal gambling and related criminal activities. Individual tracks would run for a day or a week before being raided, and then open again once the coast was clear. This was referred to as "running on the fix" and failed tracks were called "bloomers." It is believed that Smith originally envisioned basing his profits entirely on 99-cent gate receipts, but soon realized that gambling would attract bigger crowds. Rumors of drugged dogs and fixed races only grew, and early tracks gained unsavory reputations because of their perceived involvement with mobsters.

Perceptions aside, a bid to recognize dog racing as a legal activity was brought before the U.S. Supreme Court in 1927. Following the passage of a statute authorizing so-called "regular" race meetings in the state of Kentucky, O.P. Smith and his partners had opened a 4,000-seat, $50,000 facility in Erlanger. It was found that horse tracks qualified under the new law, but dog tracks did not. Similarly, it would be future Supreme Court Chief Justice Earl Warren, the then-attorney general of California, who would block the growth of dog racing in his state. The original Blue Star track in Emeryville had been shuttered after three seasons in 1922, but multiple tracks had succeeded it; all of which Warren successfully closed down by 1939.

Florida became the first place to allow dog tracks to operate legally, after lawmakers passed a pari-mutuel bill over Governor Doyle E. Carlton's veto in 1931. By 1935, there were ten licensed tracks in operation. According to the *Tallahassee Democrat*, the Governor later said he had refused a $100,000 bribe to sign the legislation. Oregon and Massachusetts became the next states to approve dog racing, in 1933 and 1934 respectively. Bay State Governor Joseph Buell Ely, a Republican, signed an emergency bill in Massachusetts authorizing horse racing in spite of the fact that dog racing was also included. Setting his personal objections to the latter aside, he chose to ignore the rebuke of his party in hopes of finding new sources of revenue during the Great Depression.

Democrat Governor Herbert H. Lehman of New York was also no fan of dog racing, and vetoed legislation presented to him in 1937. The State Racing Commission had advised that dog racing was an invitation to fraud, opposed to the best interests of sports, and particularly detrimental to the existing enterprise of horse racing. In the neighboring state of New Jersey, lawmakers approved a temporary dog racing authorization in 1934, but the state Supreme Court struck it down as unconstitutional a year later. In 1939, Arizona became the fourth state to legalize greyhound racing.

Early days of dog racing at Wonderland Greyhound Park
(Frank O'Brien/The Boston Globe via Getty Images)

Although church groups and both civic and humane organizations rallied in opposition, the new industry expanded, with Colorado and South Dakota legalizing dog racing in 1949. Eight years later, Arkansas authorized greyhound racing, and that state's Southland Greyhound Corporation was among the six new American tracks to open during the 1950s. Southland's debut was marred by the electrocution of a greyhound during a promotional race, which added to the bitter opposition of local media to the new track. For years, Memphis newspapers would not accept paid advertisements from the facility.

Referred to as the Sport of Queens, perhaps in reference to Queen Elizabeth I's promotion of greyhound coursing in the sixteenth century, dog racing sought to promote itself as elite, glamorous, and on a par with its traditional competitor, horse racing. In Florida, racetracks emphasized the "sun and fun" to be had at their facilities. Beauty pageant winners, baseball stars, and famous celebrities like Joe DiMaggio, Babe Ruth, Lou Gehrig, Burt Reynolds, Janet Leigh, Tony Curtis, and even Old Blue Eyes, Frank Sinatra, made multiple appearances at dog tracks in the Sunshine State. In 1958, Sinatra filmed a movie about a dog track gambler at the Flagler Kennel Club and a year later, he appeared on the cover of the Greyhound Racing Record along with a woman newly crowned the "Queen of American Greyhound Racing." Beside them was the winning dog in a race named after the famous singer. Tracks in other states also attracted celebrity visits. Talk show host Merv Griffin was pictured at Multnomah Greyhound Park in Oregon and both John Wayne and Paul Newman made appearances at Arizona's Tucson Greyhound Park.

Even before legalization, O.P. Smith created an organization to market dog racing. The International Greyhound Racing Association (AGTOA), though never actually international, was formed in 1926 in Miami. In 1946, Florida track owners united to form the American Greyhound Track Owners Association, which later welcomed owners from across the country. It published the *Greyhound Racing Record* and released the *American Greyhound Racing Encyclopedia* in 1963, both intended to publicize dog racing to the American public. In 1973, the National Coursing Association renamed itself the National Greyhound Association and opened its doors in Abilene, Kansas. Racing greyhounds had to be registered with the NGA in order to compete; the trade group maintained official breeding records and published *The Greyhound Review*. The most well-known promotion of dog racing was the Greyhound Hall of Fame, a museum and exhibit center also located in Abilene.

Early dog tracks, starting with Emeryville itself, offered hurdle racing as well as races of different lengths to attract audiences. Florida, Kansas, and Texas tracks, as well as some of the shuttered California, New Jersey, New York, Ohio, and Oklahoma tracks, even used monkeys as jockeys to pique interest. The unwilling riders were often shaken to death, prompting local humane societies to put a stop to this particular gimmick.

Dog tracks also offered musical entertainment, live radio broadcasts and cross-promotions with other entertainment venues, including movie theaters and even horse tracks, both to boost their popularity and to ward off complaints from neighboring businesses. However, later greyhound racing proponents would reject the opportunity to broadcast races on television for fear of losing in-person bettors. This decision put dog racing at a competitive disadvantage with horse racing, which was coincidentally legalized in the major media markets of New York and California. Lacking a mainstream audience, individual dogs were never to achieve the acclaim of champion horses like Seabiscuit or Seattle Slew. Winning greyhounds such as Mission Boy, Rural Rube, Downing, and Keefer would remain unknown to the general public, celebrated only in the record books of the NGA.

Monkeys were sometimes used as greyhound jockeys
(Bettmann via Getty Images)

In the backdrop of its push to build popularity, dog racing was always challenged to distance itself from organized crime. Joe Linsey, three-time president of the AGTOA and also a convicted bookmaker, owned the original Taunton, Massachusetts track, five Colorado tracks, and the Lincoln, Rhode Island facility. Gangsters Meyer Lansky, Bugsy Siegel, Lucky Luciano, and Al Capone were said to have interests in tracks such as the Hawthorne track in Illinois and the Miami Beach and Hollywood Kennel Clubs of Florida. In 1950, the U.S. Senate Special Committee to Investigate Organized Crime in Interstate Commerce looked at these connections and charged that Chicago mobsters had infiltrated Florida dog track operations, controlled the state racing commission, and funneled illegal contributions to politicians.

Rumors of organized crime also surrounded Emprise, a Buffalo, New York-based company that owned dog track interests stretching across the country. In 1972, it faced felony fines for racketeering and conspiring to conceal ownership in a Nevada casino. Four years later, an Arizona Republic reporter named Don Bolles was fatally injured by a car bomb while investigating related activities, accusing Emprise of murdering him as he lay mortally wounded. The company was never charged in the assassination, and a greyhound breeder named John Harvey Adamson was instead sent up for the crime. Emprise would later change its name to Delaware North.

More conflict arose within the industry itself when "dogmen," the breeders, handlers, kennel operators, and others working at dog tracks, went on strike several times. In 1935, 1948, 1957, and again in 1975, they demanded greater fairness in bookings and a higher cut of the bets made on their dogs. The 1948 strikes were led by the short-lived Greyhound Owners Benevolent Association, modeled after similar groups working successfully in the horse industry. In 1975, multiple strikes were tried in several states, but none were successful. The "Flagler 18" was a group of dogmen associated with the Miami track. The court ordered them to return to work; when they refused and found themselves locked up behind bars. Twenty-three greyhound owners also picketed in New Hampshire, and in Arizona they threatened to kill twenty-five dogs a day until track management would agree to their demands. State Attorney General Bruce Babbitt obtained a restraining order to block the killings and described the failed ploy as "senseless, repulsive, inhumane, unjust [and] immoral."

These strikes attracted public interest, and the media responded with intense coverage beginning in the 1970s. While questions had always been raised about the underfed appearance of racing greyhounds, increased media attention would now focus on the humane issues surrounding racing itself. In September 1975, the *National Enquirer* published an article, "Greyhound Racing—Where Brutality and Greed Finish Ahead of Decency," causing alarm among industry proponents such as Gary Guccione. A one-time writer for the National Coursing Association, he had become the Executive Director of the NGA. The first major televised report came from a young investigative reporter named Geraldo Rivera. His first-hand look at the training and coursing of Kansas greyhounds with live lures aired in June 1978 on the premiere episode of ABC's *20/20*. Concerns were then raised in Washington DC, where U.S. Senators Birch Bayh and Bob Dole introduced a bill to make it a federal crime to engage in live lure training. Their proposed amendment to the Animal Welfare Act was never to become law, amid promises from the industry to police itself.

Exposés continued to air on programs like *Inside Edition*, while national magazines including *Life, Reader's Digest, and Ladies' Home Journal* featured full-length articles on the cruelty of dog racing. The discovery of one hundred dead ex-racing greyhounds, shot and buried in an abandoned lemon grove in Chandler, Arizona, was brought to light by the *Arizona Republic*. A greyhound burial ground serving the Hinsdale track of New Hampshire was uncovered by *Fox News*. On January 3, 1993, *National Geographic* aired a program entitled "Running for Their Lives." In it, the wanton killing of unprofitable greyhounds was revealed, causing racetrack executive Fred Havenick to admit on camera that his industry needed to be cleaned up. Decades later, Fred's son Izzy would play a key role in ending greyhound racing in his home state of Florida.

The overbreeding of greyhounds had become a problem in the dog racing world very early on. A 1952 article in the *Greyhound Racing Record* calculated that fewer than thirty percent of greyhounds born on breeding farms were usable for racing. A May 1958 article published in the popular men's magazine *Argosy* quoted one kennel operator and breeder as explaining that there were three types of greyhounds in a litter: those who race, those who breed, and those who are destroyed. The cover featured four racing greyhounds with the question, "Must these dogs die?" In the 1970s, as more and more states authorized dog racing and the industry grew, the NGA's approval of artificial insemination techniques facilitated greyhound breeding, making it easier and less expensive to produce litters. Small farms had about forty breeding dogs, medium-size facilities averaged about one hundred, and the larger facilities bred hundreds of dogs every year. Thousands of racing dogs were surrendered to Massachusetts Society for the Prevention of Cruelty to Animals shelters as late as 1985, humanely destroyed for a fee of $3 each. In 1990, the director of Arizona's Maricopa County shelter reported killing up to 500 greyhounds each year, all surrendered by greyhound breeders and racers who ordered them destroyed. Her plans to build another county pound to save the greyhounds fell through. Worse still, some kennel owners continued to feel that it was not only expedient, but humane to just shoot unwanted greyhounds between the eyes and be done with them.

With media attention intensifying, the industry formed the American Greyhound Council in 1987 to promote the adoption of ex-racers and lead much-needed damage control efforts. A joint project of the AGTOA and NGA, the AGC also put in place the industry's first inspection system for racing and breeding kennels. A "Greyhound Rescue Association" had been launched the year before in Cambridge, Massachusetts by anti-racing activist Hugh Geoghegan, and the AGC followed with its own "Greyhound Pets of America" chapters, requiring members to be "racing neutral." Independent organizations like USA Defenders of Greyhounds were opened in 1988, followed by the National Greyhound Adoption Program in 1989. Where there had been just twenty adoption groups nationwide in these early days, there were nearly three hundred by the mid-2000s. Greyhounds were welcomed into homes all across the country, many adopters pointing out that their dogs were "rescued."

While these controversies raged, greyhound racing continued to expand. In the 1970s and 1980s, it was legalized in the twelve additional states of Alabama, Connecticut, Idaho, Iowa, Kansas, New Hampshire, Nevada, Rhode Island, Texas, Vermont, West Virginia, and Wisconsin. Thankfully, lawmakers in some states, like Montana, resisted and refused to permit the activity. Similarly, voters in the state of California rejected two initiatives intended to legalize dog racing. The final 1976 proposal, known as Proposition 13, was brought by George Hardie of the Golden State Greyhound Association. It was crushed at the ballot box by a margin of 25%-75%. In an open letter published in *The Greyhound Review*, he had urged the national industry to support him, but to no avail. As the industry would discover decades later in Florida, thirteen appeared to be its unlucky number.

By 1991 greyhound racing had expanded to nearly seventy operational dog tracks in nineteen states, making it the sixth largest spectator sport in the country. This pinnacle was short lived, though, and the industry quickly faced intense competition from an explosion of state lotteries, tribal casinos, and casino-style gambling opportunities at the tracks themselves. During hearings for the Indian Gaming Regulatory Act of 1988, the NGA expressed interest in joining forces with Native American Tribes; but the AGTOA stepped in and testified before Congress that such a combination would allow criminal elements to infiltrate tribal communities. It seemed that track owners were more than willing to remind lawmakers of old-time dog racing's association with organized crime in order to insulate their business from unwanted competition.

This divide between track owners and greyhound breeders also meant that the dogmen were often denied many of the economic benefits the industry had to offer. In the late 1980s, track owners won approval to share signals and take wagers on each other's races. "Simulcasting" was a tool that helped the industry, but in the end the dogmen were excluded. In 1989, they attempted to pass a federal bill to secure a greater share of wagering proceeds and to have veto power over inter-track agreements. H.R. 3429, the Interstate Greyhound Racing Act, was modeled after the successful Interstate Horse Racing Act of 1978 but was doomed to fail once the AGTOA came to oppose it. Track owners challenged the measure as unnecessary federal regulation and criticized it as a "private relief" bill for greyhound owners. Representing the NGA, Gary Guccione testified that fewer than half of his members could even cover their costs of operation—but relief was not to come.

The greed of track owners, paired with years of industry mistakes, created an opportunity for the animal welfare community, but movement leaders hesitated. Investigations by advocates like Ann Church, Bob Baker, and Laura Bevan of the Humane Society of the United States had uncovered live lure training and often caught violators in the act. Despite this groundbreaking work, no established animal protection groups opposed greyhound racing. The American Society for the Prevention of Cruelty to Animals (ASPCA) even accepted major donations from the industry to be used for adoption, an arrangement the industry trumpeted for maximum public relations benefit. Some early voices, including Hugh Geoghegan, warned animal groups that they were being co-opted and abdicating their responsibility to confront the dog racers. Although Geoghegan's pleas fell on deaf ears, change was about to come. A local grassroots movement, led by people who had nothing to lose and were not afraid to stand up to powerful racetrack owners, was about to emerge. Everyday citizens were ready to give the dogs a much-needed voice.

CHAPTER 2

A FEW HIGHLY COMPETITIVE DOGS

"It hardly seems worth it to me to go through that process of breeding and killing the ones that can't compete, just to have the sport."

—Idaho Governor Phil Batt

In 1989, animal protection group In Defense of Animals came to learn that the U.S. Army planned to kill 118 former ex-racing greyhounds at its Presidio laboratories in San Francisco. The dogs would have a piece of leg bone removed and then replaced by a bone-mending compound. After two months of healing, the dogs would be killed, and their limbs subjected to stress tests. IDA learned of the plans and alerted Congresswoman Barbara Boxer, who launched inquiries. The group also paired up with a local sighthound rescuer named Susan Netboy. Through a series of demonstrations, legal maneuvers, and news exposés, the coalition was able to halt the program and secure freedom for the surviving dogs. Two years later in 1991, Netboy formed the Greyhound Protection League to advocate for racing dogs full-time.

Over the next decade, the Greyhound Protection League led the first national movement against greyhound racing. It was a grassroots effort that received only token support from mainstream animal groups. Netboy cultivated an extensive network of industry informants, who provided her with inside information on dog racing throughout the country. She was a regular contributor to the national anti-racing newsletter, *Greyhound Network News*, which had been launched in 1992 by Joan Eidinger in Arizona. Netboy was particularly skilled at exposing the use of greyhounds in research laboratories. In 1998 she helped publicize a major scandal in which 2,600 ex-racers were donated for terminal lab experiments at the Colorado State University veterinary school over a three-year period. The *Rocky Mountain News* reported on the public outcry that led to the end of the program. A few years later, in the Spring of 2000, the *Wisconsin State Journal*, the *Des Moines Register*, and the *Chicago Sun-Times* were among the newspapers that reported on the sale of one thousand greyhounds to the Guidant cardiac research lab in Minnesota. NGA member Daniel Shonka, who accepted the dogs on the premise of placing them for adoption, instead sold them to the laboratory for $400 each. In 2006, history repeated itself when the *Denver Post* reported that Richard Favreau, who had also released dogs to CSU, received $28,000 to adopt out approximately two hundred greyhounds, but could only account for a handful of them. As with all of these cases, Netboy worked to publicize the situation, creating a public relations nightmare for the dog racing industry.

Meanwhile, interest in greyhound racing waned in the face of competition from other forms of gambling. Tracks provided fewer and fewer tax dollars, and some states began taking a loss on the activity. The 1990s bankruptcies of the Key West, Interstate, Green Mountain, Black Hills, Yuma, Fox Valley, Sodrac, Coeur D'Alene, Biscayne, Greenetrack, Wisconsin Dells, and Waterloo tracks across nine states signaled weakness in the industry and ended dog racing entirely in several states. Meanwhile the grassroots coalition Netboy and others had built began to achieve its first political victories, as states began turning back the clock on greyhound racing. Over the course of a decade, the authorization for pari-mutuel wagering on live dog racing was repealed in Vermont, Idaho, and Nevada, and preemptive measures to outlaw dog racing were passed in Maine, Virginia, Washington, and North Carolina. These latter campaigns, along with a subsequent push in Pennsylvania, were prophylactic in nature, designed to stave off attempts to introduce dog racing in the first place.

These early advances were frequently led by strong women. *Greyhound Network News* documented the work of Evelyn Jones, Sherry Cotner, and Ellie Sciurba in leading successful petition drives followed by legislative action. Vermont's "Gator Bill" came to pass after Massachusetts Society for the Prevention of Cruelty to Animals shelter manager John Perrault presented his photographs of dead greyhounds to lawmakers. The greyhounds pictured were among the truckloads he was asked to destroy once the racing season ended at the Green Mountain track each year. Scotti Devens of Save the Greyhound Dogs! and Greyhound Rescue Vermont lobbied for the bill that was ultimately signed by Governor Howard Dean. Lawmakers in Idaho acted after documentation surfaced about the electrocution, shootings, and throat slashings of unwanted dogs. Both the Greyhound Protection League and Greyhound Rescue of Idaho advocated for Governor Phil Batt to sign a racing prohibition into law. An avowed dog lover, he signed the bill with his poodle-schnauzer on his lap, remarking that "dog racing depends upon selecting a few highly competitive dogs out of a large group. It hardly seems worth it to me to go through that process of breeding and killing the ones that can't compete, just to have the sport."

When the industry faced these initial setbacks, it did not reflect on fundamental problems that had festered for years or consider any reforms of consequence. Instead, track owners and greyhound breeders focused on a singular obsession that would dominate the policy debate for years to come, the legalization of slot machines at racetracks. Referred to as the "crack cocaine of gambling" by opponents, these gambling devices were thought to offer new hope for remaining tracks, but ultimately became a double-edged sword, pitting track owners against dogmen. As tracks in states like Iowa, Rhode Island, and West Virginia were initially granted casino-type gambling, they were also required to share their profits with live racing interests. This enhanced a divide that later resulted in track owners joining with greyhound advocates to pass bills to repeal statutory dog racing mandates and "decouple" live racing from other gambling at the facilities. As this slot machine fight raged, the industry continued to decline, and grassroots opposition intensified.

In 1997, the fight to end dog racing entered a new phase when a small group of Massachusetts animal rights advocates joined togcthcr to challenge the industry. Like their ancestors before them, they were ready to start their own revolution. In the mid-1990s, advocates like Libby Frattaroli, Steve Baer, and Anna Piccolo had begun to call public attention to the cruelty occurring at Bay State dog tracks. Christine learned of their efforts and joined in. Their unsophisticated but intense protest movement also found an ally in Republican State Representative Shaun Kelly of Berkshire County. In contrast to similar pushes in other states, his legislation aimed to shut down viable, operational facilities that wielded immense political influence. The Kelly bill gave advocates a beacon to organize around, but despite a strong lobbying push, other lawmakers refused to support him in his bid to help the greyhounds. This left both sides at a stalemate, with the industry slowly dying but still deeply entrenched. Dog track barons Charlie Sarkis and George Carney, who were said to be top political donors on a par with corporate giants such as Polaroid and Genzyme, successfully used their decades-long relationships with Beacon Hill leadership to avoid public scrutiny.

New England was the crown jewel of American greyhound racing, and for decades had been tightly controlled by Carney, who now owned Raynham Park in southeastern Massachusetts, and Sarkis, who ran the iconic Wonderland just north of Boston. These two strongmen had been locked in a pugnacious rivalry that always seemed to be on the verge of violence. At one point, Sarkis told the state Racing Commission that his life was in danger because of "mobster" Carney.

Sarkis himself was no stranger to organized crime. His father, Abe, was a known bookmaker and a reputed associate of the Patriarca crime family who had reportedly survived at least one assassination attempt. Despite this family history, Charlie was approved to purchase Revere's Wonderland Greyhound Park in 1977. Thirteen years later, forty people including his father along with the track's general manager, were indicted on charges of running an illegal gaming operation right on the premises. Charlie himself was not prosecuted and later lamented, "It is what it is. My father was my father." In addition to Wonderland, Sarkis also briefly operated a harness horse racing track called the Bay State Raceway. Six years after he leased the Foxboro property, however, it was purchased by Bob Kraft who quickly moved to terminate the arrangement.

Charlie Sarkis and George Carney testify on Beacon Hill, December 18, 2007 (AP Photo/Josh Reynolds, © 2007 AP)

Charles F. Sarkis grew up in Milton, Massachusetts as an only child. He bought his first restaurant in 1964, and in the ensuing decades built a small business empire. A tall man, he wore dark, pin-striped suits and was very charismatic—and equally combustible! He definitely liked to play the agitator. One example of this came in the fall of 2000, when he debated Dr. Jill Hopfenbeck on the Howie Carr radio show. As one of the spokespersons to end dog racing, Hopfenbeck was deeply knowledgeable and had cared for thousands of former racing dogs. When Sarkis arrived at the station, he could barely contain his rage. Dr. Hopfenbeck and Sarkis argued bitterly for the entire hour, continuing their debate through the commercial breaks. During one off-air moment, Sarkis bragged that greyhound racing was regulated by the State Police, and Jill responded that everyone knew the unit was there to prevent the infiltration of organized crime, not to protect the dogs. Sarkis erupted, and the ensuing verbal mêlée made headlines the following day. A few years later, Carey found himself in an elevator alone with both Sarkis and George Carney. Although Sarkis was reportedly suffering from a condition that made it difficult for him to remember faces, he recognized Carey immediately and began ranting, "I'm going to kill you." Carney tried to calm Sarkis, reminding him that a State House elevator was not the time or place for such business.

George L. Carney, Jr. was a barreling, gregarious man with a shock of pure white hair. He had grown up in Ireland, and during a 2000 radio debate, told Carey and greyhound advocate Laurel Finucan that his father had taken him to cockfights as a child, and that greyhound racing and cock fighting were both great! Carney projected the image of a benevolent patriarch but was in fact far more ruthless than Sarkis. In 1981, in a demonstration of pure power, George had used his connections to force a consolidation with a second, nearby dog racing permit, and won the right to have more race dates than his rival, Charlie.

Sarkis and Carney were formidable opponents and wielded immense control over the Massachusetts legislature. Although the Kelly bill had given the greyhound movement life, it would never overcome their influence. A new approach was needed, one that could circumvent Beacon Hill completely. One such avenue existed, *via* the citizens' initiative process, but it was so extraordinarily difficult that no grassroots group had successfully used it in decades. In short, greyhound advocates had to take the greyhound problem directly to voters—and were ready to give it their best shot, even though they would be facing nearly impossible odds.

CHAPTER 3

SEEDS OF ITS OWN DESTRUCTION

"My priorities weren't right. I decided that if I ever walked again, my life was going to be different. I was going to look beyond myself."

—Christine A. Dorchak

Christine Dorchak was born in Plainfield, New Jersey in 1966, the first child of a chemical engineer named Tom and a multi-talented stay-at-home mom named Lillie. Each gave her a strong sense of independence and integrity, one by inadvertence and the other by way of example.

Christine was raised very strictly, always made to understand that she had a duty to succeed, to make her parents proud. She was to get top grades in school, play a musical instrument, and participate in athletics and more— all with the goal of being admitted to a top university. She worked part-time at her father's start-up consultancy beginning at the age of twelve. She cleaned the house each morning to earn her lunch money and at the age of fifteen, got her first outside job as a "Ranch Hand" at fast food restaurant Roy Rogers. She went on to work at an energy company run by the family of Governor Tom Kean, and then a law firm, both in Bridgewater, New Jersey. She knew she was supposed to do everything she could to create the "perfect résumé" so that she could eventually enter a top profession and make everyone proud.

Valedictorian of her class and member of the middle school orchestra, drama club, and choir, Christine was as an honors student in high school as well. She studied two languages and was French Club president while also winning Varsity letters in cross country and track. She wrote for her school newspaper and was a statistician for the basketball team. This tough regimen would benefit Christine in ways not imagined at the time, but in truth, it was also a mechanism for avoiding a sometimes-uneasy home life. In fact, just as Christine was about to start her junior year, her parents separated. For the next two years, each would take turns living in the family home with Christine and her younger brother.

This difficult time ended when her father moved away permanently, and her mother and brother relocated to a smaller home nearby. Mom would rejoin the work force and, among other pursuits, start her own catering business, open a gourmet food shop, and then go on to become a newspaper editor before obtaining her paralegal degree. She was Christine's role model in every way, teaching her that no matter what life presented, there was a way to grow as a person and to be self-sufficient. Thankfully, Christine had been accepted to Boston University and, now in 1984, was able to continue pursuing her dreams thanks to scholarships and financial aid. Christine would lose her financial aid twice and spend alternate years back in New Jersey, studying at Rutgers. But she was determined to get her degree in Boston and after six years, graduated with a Bachelor of Science degree in Broadcast Journalism.

Throughout her college years, Christine had supported herself by working in law firms, at a modem company, at the front desk of the Crown Plaza Hotel, at the B.U. bookstore, and by scooping ice cream at world-famous Emack and Bolio's on Newbury Street. But now with her diploma in hand, she fully intended to become a foreign correspondent for *CNN* or work at one of the major television networks. All her hard work was about to pay off!

But then life took a turn. Early one morning, while Christine was walking her dog Kelsey, the two were hit by a speeding train. Kelsey had managed to pull them slightly off course, thus preventing a head-on collision and likely saving their lives. When Christine awoke from her coma, her first words were, "How's Kelsey?" Thankfully, though Kelsey had suffered a broken hip the day of the accident, she was to live until the age of fifteen, dying just a few days after Christine finished law school in 2005. Facing terrible memory loss and physical disability, Christine realized she had to forego her TV dreams. But with these challenges came a new sense of purpose. She promised that if she should ever recover from her injuries and walk again, she would devote her life to helping dogs.

Christine's mother Lillie, like her mother before her, had always loved dogs, squirrels, rabbits—all animals, in fact. This compassion was something that she passed on to both of her children. One of the first professional pictures taken of baby Christine shows her with her mother's beloved black poodle, Mandy. Christine's Italian grandmother also had a poodle, whom she named "Tina" after her new granddaughter. Dogs were simply part of the Scilipoti and Dorchak family. When she was a teenager, Christine found a dog whom she named Bunny. This little beagle had run away from a nearby hunter and Christine hid her in the basement, fearing that her father would make her give up the frightened dog. But when her father discovered Bunny, he was convinced to let her stay. Christine's brother, Tom, had already rescued a beagle named Oliver from the same hunter, so fair was fair!

When she left for college, Christine again hid Bunny, this time in her Boston-area apartment where no dogs were allowed. She simply could not fathom life without her Best Friend. Then, after losing Bunny to cancer in 1991, Christine decided to make a memorial donation to the Lowell Humane Society. With only $5 to give, she and her brother entered the shelter to find just one dog, sitting by herself, in a cage. She was a huge, furry puppy with gleaming eyes, full of life—but her time was up. Christine begged for Kelsey to be kept alive a little bit longer, promising to come back with the money needed to adopt her. Over the next week, she raised $45 by collecting discarded cans along the city streets and by scavenging the bleachers after a Boston College football game. The following Saturday, she returned to Lowell, paid the fee in full, and took Kelsey home to Brighton. This beautiful Black Russian Terrier whose life Christine had saved, would go on to return the favor almost exactly a year later in 1992.

Even after being released from the hospital and then staying at a specialized rehabilitation facility in 1993, Christine was unable to care for herself following her accident. She was taken back home to New Jersey, where her mother set out to help her regain her memory and confidence, and to restore some of the knowledge that had been wiped away by the train's impact. This was a difficult and scary time, as Christine felt lost in a world she no longer knew. The only thing she could truly remember was her love for Kelsey; this love gave her the strength to learn to walk and talk and take care of herself again. Whether it was reading a clock, tying her shoes, learning how to wash clothes, or relearning world history, Mom taught her as much as she could and dropped her off at the library each day to study. Christine would pore through the encyclopedia, look up famous people like Christopher Columbus, and try to regain a sense of the world. Everything was new!

With this novel perspective, Christine gained a fresh outlook on life and had the rare opportunity to start again. Perhaps she had been on the wrong track, so to speak, in 1992? What was life all about anyway? After reading Peter Singer's seminal book, *Animal Liberation*, Christine believed she had the answer. Here was a way to repay her debt to Kelsey and to restart her life. She would become an animal advocate. By 1999, Christine had fully recovered from her accident and become a full-fledged activist. She attended multiple fur and circus protests each month; she promoted vegetarianism at outreach tables, regularly wrote letters-to-the-editor to the *Boston Globe*, and even worked as the research director of an anti-vivisection society.

Christine and Kelsey commemorating National Homeless Animals Day at the Massachusetts State House in Boston, 1997 (Christine A. Dorchak)

In 2000, the final piece fell into place. Christine decided to become a lawyer. The idea of a head-injured woman going to law school seemed like a stretch, but Christine reasoned that she had known and worked for a lot of lawyers who didn't seem exceptionally gifted—so if they could do it, so could she! A fellow animal advocate loaned her the money to hire a tutor and take the LSAT. She passed the test and was fortunate enough to win a full scholarship to the New England School of Law. But then life took another turn. . .

Carey Theil was born in 1978 into a world of chaos. His mother Connie suffered from addiction when he was a child, and came from a dysfunctional family of alcoholics, religious zealots, and ruffians.

Despite these obstacles Connie was deeply independent, creative, and dedicated to social justice. When Carey was a young child his mother took him to late night *avant-garde* art shows at the Pirate Gallery in Denver, introduced him to foreign films and dreamed of writing an epic novel about her life.

He was also the first Theil to break the cycle of self-destruction that had seeped down through the generations like poison spreading through the roots of a tree. Carey's father was a mythical figure, a man who was both intelligent and socially conscious, but had vanished soon after his son was born. Carey was raised to be outspoken. He was given few rules to follow and always taught to think for himself. He wrote poetry at a young age, was a frequent target of bullying and often gravitated to other children who were also outsiders in one way or another.

When he entered high school, Carey tested so well that he was placed in an elite magnet program called Research Scholars, located at Marshall High School. His test scores more than compensated for middling grades and regular truancy. During his freshman year he joined the school chess club and quickly became consumed with the ancient game. But within a few months, Carey became disenchanted with the educational system when his reports of cheating by his fellow students went unpunished. He retreated into the school drama program, where he briefly found a home among other misfits. But even this would not last. So by his sophomore year, he found himself at the Metropolitan Learning Center for troubled students. Carey did better at MLC, which provided him with more freedom and required a long trip across the city each day. But like the Marshall drama program, this too was unsustainable. By his third year Carey left school completely and led a nomadic life, sleeping on a different friend's couch each night. Carey became deeply introspective and studied chess theory for days on end. He discovered the writings of Hermann Hesse and Fyodor Dostoyevsky, wrote poetry, and tried to find his path.

Carey plays chess, 2002 (Tony Cortizas, Jr.)

Meanwhile, his mother awoke to the plight of animals after seeing captive elephants at the local zoo. She became the president of a local animal rights group and had long conversations with Carey about the exploitation of animals. She volunteered for a successful 1994 ballot measure that banned the hound hunting of bears and cougars and prohibited a particularly cruel hunting practice known as bear baiting. When hunting groups tried to repeal the mountain lion ban two years later, Carey was hired to work on a campaign to protect the ballot question. Sixteen years old, he was truly starting on the ground level. When he arrived at work for the first time, coalition manager Paul Van Dyke showed him how to do data entry, telling Carey that he would try him out for a day. Carey worked as hard as he could so that one day became two, then a week, then the remainder of the campaign.

One day, an executive with the Humane Society of the United States named Wayne Pacelle visited the office. He carried an air of great authority, and everyone seemed intimidated by him. Wayne was a rising star in the animal rights movement and a leading proponent of the idea that animal protection should become a mainstream political movement. He had broken through a few years earlier by helping pass a key California measure that outlawed the trophy hunting of mountain lions. Following that victory, he began passing ballot measures on a wide range of animal protection issues, work that would continue for decades. Carey was not immediately impressed but came to understand that Wayne's philosophy was right. He had previously been skeptical of politics, and at one point even told his mother that although he believed in animal rights as a concept, real change could never actually happen. Now he too became convinced of the idea that justice for animals could in fact be won through a political struggle.

At roughly the same time, Wayne's influence also reached Christine. She had read his article about the cruelty of dog racing in *Animals' Agenda Magazine*, and this was part of what led her to host her own animal rights TV show called *"Animal Agenda."* She had started out airing live in Cambridge with an open mic but went on to broadcast recorded programming statewide with the help of skilled producer Diana Cartier. Diana was also one of the principals of local animal rights organization CEASE, whose president at the time was a young animal rights attorney named Steven Wise.

After the Oregon ballot question to legalize hound hunting was happily defeated, Carey felt directionless. He took the seven hundred dollars that he had earned and decided to travel by bus and train across the country. He was awestruck by the vast nation before him and kept detailed journals in which he described vast plains, colossal mountain ranges, and glittering cities, as well as the idiosyncratic people he met along the way. He walked down snow filled boulevards beneath immense skyscrapers in Chicago and crossed a narrow bridge over Lake Pontchartrain in the middle of the night. One morning, while riding on a Greyhound bus, he awoke at dawn to a hot pink sky. This was his first glimpse of Florida, the place he would later come to know as the heart of dog racing.

The following year Oregon hunters tried yet again to overturn the will of the voters and allow hound hunting, this time *via* a bill in the state legislature. Along with other advocates, Carey was asked to testify against the proposal. He went to a used clothing store, bought a polyester suit, and took a bus to the state capitol in Salem. He didn't know how to tie a necktie, so a fellow passenger volunteered to help him.

Wearing his Goodwill suit and sporting a pencil mustache, Carey showed up at the hearing to protect Mountain Lions. He gave fiery testimony, and afterwards was pulled aside by Republican State Senator Ted Ferrioli, a conservative timber company executive. Ferrioli laughed at Carey and told him his testimony had been highly inappropriate. Despite this admonishment, and for reasons that remain unclear to this day, Ferrioli began to tutor Carey at the Capitol. This invaluable insight empowered Carey to fight for the animals. Carey gained a second mentor when he befriended State Senator Tom Wilde, a tall, thin man with a thick beard. Wilde was an outsider who had spent years traveling the country to research and write a book about violin makers. He was thoughtful, eccentric, and had been elected under bizarre circumstances. Following an argument with his wife as manager of her Senate campaign, Wilde lived up to his name and took out nominating papers to run against her. His win made global headlines.

Wilde served only a single term and was ostracized by both parties. He joked to Carey that he was a caucus of one, and it was easy to get appointments with him because he received fewer requests than any other lawmaker. Nonetheless Wilde understood the political culture in Salem, helping Carey to navigate through its menagerie of ideologues, hustlers, and deal makers. Carey visited Wilde regularly and listened to the Senator vent about a hodgepodge of topics that ranged from who was sleeping with whom, to which bills would be brought to the floor by leadership, and of course his continued laments that neither the Democrats nor the Republicans welcomed him. Wilde had a passing interest in the animal protection bills Carey worked on, but more importantly taught him that lawmakers are people, with their own ambitions and quirks.

Just weeks after he testified in Salem that first time, Carey began to have success. Animal advocates were largely absent in Salem, and there were a host of bills being brought by animal exploiters that called out for opposition. Carey began tracking them himself, making the bus trip from Portland as often as he could. He prepared his own testimony, sought and received meeting appointments, and started to count votes on anti-animal proposals. During this period Carey met Republican State Senator John Lim, for whom he would later briefly work as a legislative aide. Carey also became a close confidant of Susan Netboy, founder of the Greyhound Protection League. Susan worked with Carey and his mother on a stakeout of the local Multnomah track at the end of the racing season in 1999. Susan had learned that a greyhound handler planned to transport dozens of dogs across the country in a broken-down Ryder truck. Unfortunately, they were unable to prevent this reckless act, which led to the death of six dogs.

On the final night of the legislative session, Carey and his mother opposed a bill to give Multnomah Greyhound Park a multimillion-dollar subsidy. They rushed to the capitol, and as day became night, urged Senators to vote against the proposal. They fought tooth and nail, attempting to counter every move by the powerful lobbying team that represented the track. As midnight approached, the bill came up for a vote. Senators passionately argued both for and against, before Tom Wilde and other Senators cast decisive No votes, narrowly defeating the dog racing subsidy. The Theils drove home, ebullient and amazed that they had won.

The next morning, however, they awakened to a great shock. In the middle of the night the bill had been reconsidered, and four Senators, including Tom Wilde and future Governor Kate Brown, had switched sides and approved the subsidy. There now remained just one final way to defeat the dog racing bill: securing a veto from Governor John Kitzhaber. Public libraries had been requesting funding in the final hours of the legislative session and been rebuffed. Carey connected this with the greyhound fight, sprang into action, and quickly organized a press conference on the front steps of the central library in downtown Portland. This bold move attracted the attention of Reverend Tom Grey, founder of the National Coalition Against Legalized Gambling.

A Methodist minister and Vietnam War veteran who had led—and lost—soldiers in battle, Reverend Grey had spent years traveling across the country fighting casinos. With virtually zero financial resources, he had repeatedly triumphed in seemingly unwinnable fights by mobilizing grassroots volunteers and leveraging free press. Tom was incorruptible and clever, and had become inspired as a college student after spending an evening with Dr. Martin Luther King, Jr. Tom first fought the gambling industry when a riverboat casino was proposed on the Fox River in his home state of Illinois. That local dustup became a statewide fight, then a national mission after Tom was featured on *60 Minutes* and profiled in *Time Magazine*. Humble to his core, Tom hated this newfound fame. After his *CBS* interview aired, he phoned the producers and asked that it never run again. When the astonished journalists asked why, Tom said that the segment had brought him no additional support, but instead had inundated him with new requests for help, giving him far more work than he had the ability to take on! Despite his heavy load, or perhaps because of it, Tom would go on to become a key mentor for us. His practical and savvy advice deeply influenced our campaigning and philosophical approach. Tom reminded us that exploitative industries contain within themselves the seeds of their own destruction, and that the power of everyday people can win the day. He told us that "the situation is the boss." He also told us "never to leave the field." This remarkably simple, yet powerful perspective is what has grounded us and helped provide the patience and faith needed to persevere in some of our most difficult times.

Carey's 1997 library press conference was well-attended, and Tom Wilde made headlines when he signed a letter asking Governor Kitzhaber to reject the track's bill. Of course, Wilde was portrayed as the ultimate flip flopper: voting against the subsidy bill, changing his vote to help it pass in the middle of the night, then urging the Governor to veto it. After a tremendous public outcry, the Governor killed the racetrack subsidy. Incredibly, the Theils had prevailed after all.

In the years which followed Carey became one of the leading young chess players in the country, reaching top 100 status in his age group. He also worked closely with legendary socialite, journalist, and animal rights activist Paige Powell, who taught Carey how to interact with the media, while also paying him to do odd jobs. One day he would be hanging a priceless Basquiat painting depicting two chimps hugging, and the next he would be assembling a wood cabinet that had belonged to Andy Warhol! Paige was an important guide, although Carey felt sad whenever he was with her. She was still mourning the loss of many of her New York friends, including her one-time partner Jean-Michel, who had died a decade earlier.

Reverend Tom Grey, February 5, 2004
(AP Photo/M. Spencer Green, © 2004 AP)

Carey went on to fight for greyhounds in another Oregon
legislative session, and successfully defeated every bill introduced
to help dog racing interests. When the legislative session ended in
April 2000, he traveled to Los Angeles to interview with several
animal advocacy organizations, including Last Chance for Animals.
But before the interviews could happen, Carey received a call from
a man named David Vaughn about a proposed ballot question to
end greyhound racing on the east coast. David explained that he
needed to withdraw from day-to-day activities for family reasons.
His first child had just been born with a serious kidney disorder and
David's energies had to be refocused on keeping little Gus alive.

He would not abandon the volunteers, but he could no longer run things on his own. David explained the situation and urged Carey to come to Massachusetts to help them. When Carey asked when he was needed, David bought him a plane ticket for the next day.

Within hours of landing at Logan Airport, Carey was leafleting in Copley Square, along the route of the 103rd Boston Marathon. Little did he know that he must have seen Christine cross the finish line that day, and that he had just leaped headfirst into a grand adventure that would change both of their lives forever.

CHAPTER 4

THE MASSACHUSETTS MIRACLE

"Anytime you have the people up against the money and muscle of the gambling industry, bet on the people."

—Reverend Tom Grey

David Vaughn was introduced to the suffering caused by commercial dog racing through two dogs, Sebastian and Aggie. Sebastian lived for only a week after adoption. Unfortunately, the veterinarian who performed his neuter operation was not aware that greyhounds need a far lighter dose of anesthesia than other dogs, and poor Sebastian never awoke from surgery. David and his wife Janice were devastated, but one of the volunteers at the local rescue kennel thought of a way to help them and save another dog's life at the same time. Adoption advocate Robin Norton knew of a greyhound who was on the "kill list" in neighboring New Hampshire. She drove up to the track and brought Aggie home to the Vaughns. This beautiful fawn dog was the inspiration for the organization he would later call "Grey2K." It was through her that David realized he could, and should, do something to help all the other dogs facing the same cruel fate that Aggie had narrowly escaped.

Meanwhile, Robin had her own ideas. She approached David for his advice about politics and to ask how she and her fellow advocates might pass a bill to ban dog racing in Massachusetts. David turned out to be the perfect person to answer this question, as he had grown up on Beacon Hill. His grandfather had served as a state senator and chapter president of the local Republican Party, and David himself had run for Boston City Council and worked on many political contests. David told Robin the truth, that she would need to take her case directly to the voters. Admittedly, David did not know much about the citizen initiative process, but he knew enough to realize it was the only potential path for success.

Ballot initiatives are the proverbial Mount Everest of animal advocacy. Unlike the legislative process, which is designed to foster compromise, ballot questions are zero sum games. One side prevails, and the other goes down. There is no middle ground. To succeed, a group must collect hundreds of thousands of signatures from voters, survive legal challenges, and persuade millions of voters to support their cause. Because initiatives are so extraordinarily difficult, most groups won't even attempt this route without a war chest of donors at the outset. To make matters even more difficult, Massachusetts' four million voters knew very little about greyhound racing, which meant massive public outreach would be needed. When voters aren't familiar with an issue, education can be a herculean task— and it's virtually impossible to reach enough hearts and minds to make a difference without using mass media channels. Paid political ads cost a small fortune, making them all but inaccessible to small grassroots organizations.

These were the challenges David faced when he brought together a ragtag group of activists to take on the Bay State's two powerful dog tracks. He hoped to collect the necessary signatures with an all-volunteer effort, something that had not been accomplished in decades. It cannot be emphasized strongly enough that the Grey2K volunteers were a rare and determined breed. Four years earlier, Massachusetts voters had passed a ballot initiative to outlaw steel jaw leghold traps. The measure had been brought by Wayne Pacelle and the Humane Society of the United States, in partnership with the Massachusetts Society for the Prevention of Cruelty to Animals. The "Ban Cruel Traps" initiative had comfortably passed. Many of the people now fighting for greyhounds, including Christine, were veterans of this successful petition drive, which gave them irrational confidence in passing yet another voter question.

David reached out to his friend Andrew Upton, a new attorney and rising political operative in the Democratic Party. With Andrew's help, he filed the paperwork to form a political committee. He called it the "Greyhound Racing Ends Year 2000 Committee," or Grey2K for short. Interested animal advocates were invited to a meeting at the State Street offices of Andrew's law firm. Twenty people attended, including Libby Frattaroli, Anna Piccolo, Steve Baer, Beverly Alba, Laurel Finucan, and Dr. Jill Hopfenbeck. Jill had witnessed with her own eyes the abuse suffered by racing greyhounds and knew that many would be abandoned or killed when no longer useful. She was Robin's veterinarian. As a young vet student, she had been brought into a room full of dead greyhounds on gurneys, the latest batch dropped off by the local track for use at Tuft's anatomy lab. With the final addition of David's friend Doug Rubin of Viewpoint Strategies that Spring, our David v. Goliath campaign was launched.

Reflecting on that initial phase twenty years later, David marveled at the dedication of these hundreds of volunteers. Wearing sea-green t-shirts that read "Grey2K Volunteer," they put their lives on hold to collect thousands of signatures. They stood with their clipboards, pens, and signs for hours at a time, posting themselves outside supermarkets and on busy streets, at dog parks, football games, festivals, road races, yard sales, and town days. They took shifts inside malls and begged friends and family to sign on. They sacrificed their time to collect signatures not once but twice, first in the Fall of 1999 and again in the Spring of 2000, as required by law. This remarkable group of people, which included a popular mystery writer, an FBI agent, a poetry professor, a retired schoolteacher, a Vietnam War veteran, and Lynne Rayburn—daughter of TV game show host Gene Rayburn—circulated petitions throughout the week and met every Monday night to sort incoming signature pages by town and county.

Among these grassroots heroes was Daryl Elliott. He was a signature-gathering machine and the best organizer David had ever met. When Daryl turned in 1,000 signatures at the group's first meeting, David immediately recognized a leader. Daryl's discipline and focus truly complimented David's strategic and coalition-building strengths, and he was asked to join the campaign as Managing Director. This would allow David to focus on fundraising while Daryl led the petition drive and later, organized the critical public outreach effort to come. Daryl was a deeply private man who was committed to animal rights. Fortunately, he was also a ruthless organizer. The first thing he did was create a tier of county coordinators to work under him. These coordinators were responsible for driving the volunteers in their area to collect signatures and turn them in at headquarters each week. For his part, Daryl would email a list of public events to the volunteers and demand that people sign up for them. He would follow up with key people by phone, and if any of them demurred or made an excuse—citing a family obligation or doctor's appointment or, heaven forbid, a planned vacation—there would be a long moment of silence followed by a heavy sigh. That sigh was the last thing anyone ever wanted to hear!

Daryl sent folks out to pumpkin fests, parades, store-openings, movie theaters, bowling alleys and concert halls—any place where a crowd of people could be found. Fall is a glorious time in New England, and as the first foliage appeared, local signature gathering groups formed as far away as the Berkshire Mountains. Nearly a thousand volunteers managed to work together, their numbers growing each week as if by magic.

As time passed, the slow trickle of initial signatures became a steady stream. To reach the ballot, 77,000 verified signatures would have to be submitted to town clerks across the state, with no more than 25% coming from one single county. This important balance was something Daryl had to monitor as the weeks progressed. If signatures were coming in heavily from one county, volunteers would be deployed to petition in other locations. The state of Massachusetts has one of the most difficult processes for initiatives. Not only does it offer the shortest signature gathering period anywhere (nine weeks in the first round and four weeks in the second), but the Supreme Judicial Court's "stray mark rule" made things far harder. The Court required that all signatures be submitted in "pristine" condition. This meant that a petition page with a coffee stain would be rejected by state officials. This is something that professional signature gatherers build into the equation, but our all-volunteer contingent could not be expected to achieve such perfection. It was for this reason that we were advised to create a buffer and gather at least 150,000 raw voter signatures, almost twice as many as required.

Christine and Carey collect signatures at the Prudential Center, 2000
(Christine A. Dorchak)

Each page of signatures had to contain the names of people from just one city or town, so we would literally sort and lay them out alphabetically along the hallways of MIT. This would take hours and hours, owing to the 351 different municipalities in the state. We grew to know every neighborhood, village, and subdivision. It was at this time that Christine began to stand out as one of the main drivers of the campaign. Even though she was working three part-time jobs, she capitalized on her unusual schedule to carve out time to collect and sort signatures each day. On weekends, she could be found outside the Brookline Booksmith with her dog Kelsey, or in inclement weather, stationed inside the Prudential Mall in Copley Square. By the end of the petition drive, she had turned in 10% of all signatures gathered. She had come to fear Daryl's weekly status calls and having heard his heavy sigh once, never wanted to hear it again. He would demand to know where she would be and how many signatures she could be counted on to collect, and if she came in low, a full explanation was required. After one long weekend, she sorted her signatures but somehow forgot to turn them all in. It was not until the very end of the petition drive that she found a thousand signatures sitting on top of her apartment radiator. Thankfully, they had not caught fire and were still "pristine!" She immediately called Daryl to tell him the good news but, far from congratulating her, he only gave another sigh.

David is a charismatic, persuasive person and when he initially laid out the process, everyone thought it would be easy. No one knew what was in store. As the Autumn deadline neared, and the weeks remaining became mere days, joy transformed into desperation. With only two weeks to go, we had collected only half of the signatures needed by the first deadline. The prospect of falling short loomed. Terrified that the greyhounds would not reach the ballot, Christine and other key volunteers redoubled their efforts. There was no time to waste, and the number of signatures gathered so far was simply not enough. The volunteers thought about the thousands of dogs suffering in cages at Wonderland and Raynham Parks, and no one could accept the idea of failing them now. But even with this intensified push, all seemed lost. Then, an unexpected thing happened.

Out of the blue, thousands of signatures began to arrive in overflowing packages, from local businesses, vet clinics, and private individuals across the state. In total, an avalanche of more than fifty thousand signatures materialized, enough to put us over the top. This was truly a miracle! Christine and Kelsey had succeeded in collecting 15,200 signatures by themselves, a record at that time— and perhaps even now.

With the signatures in hand, we now had only a few days to hand-deliver every single signature page to the clerks of each city and town for individual verification. Volunteers took days off from work to fan out across the state and make sure every signature was counted. It was only then that we realized that we had accomplished something truly historic, and with almost no outside help. After a second (and equally intense) signature drive that Spring, we were official. A proposal to outlaw greyhound racing, now known as Question 3, would appear before the state's voters in November.

Joy over this accomplishment quickly turned to the sober reality of a difficult undertaking. Early polling was not promising. Most ballot questions look to start with a high level of support and then work hard not to lose too many points by election day. The greyhound polling was a toss-up and, given that the track owners vowed to spend whatever it took to defeat us, prospects seemed dim. Polling aside, David began visiting local and national animal protection groups to see if there was any interest in donating to his fledgling campaign. Most of the groups were polite and somewhat encouraging, but none would actually help. The Humane Society of the United States said no and the Massachusetts Society for the Prevention of Cruelty to Animals said no. Everyone said no. But then the greyhounds got lucky again.

Dr. Jill Hopfenbeck and Demi, 2000 (John Mottern/AFP via Getty Images)

Arthur Slade, the long-serving President of the Animal Rescue League of Boston, saw the potential of Grey2K. He advocated for the greyhounds before his board of directors, one of whom had a greyhound herself. A few days later, David got a phone call from Arthur that changed everything: he was pledging $100,000. Arthur said he did not predict initial success but knew that someone had to take the first step.

In between the two petition drives, Carey joined Grey2K as its first employee. He worked closely with political guru Doug Rubin, who would later lead successful campaigns to elect Senator Elizabeth Warren and Governor Deval Patrick. Doug's advice was to tell voters the story of how racing dogs live every day. He recommended that we personify the problem by letting voters see through the eyes of a single dog. Carey was skeptical of this approach, as were some steering committee members, and it was rejected. In assembling a Fall strategy, Grey2K instead followed the advice of Susan Netboy and emphasized poor industry standard practices. Unfortunately, we did not yet understand the need to localize the problem and use data that was state-specific. We argued that the national greyhound racing industry was cruel and inhumane, and that Massachusetts was tolerating and supporting a disgraceful activity. Although this was logically sound, we soon discovered that we had bitten off more than we could chew.

We were also harmed by an inadvertent mistake that had been made during the signature drive by grassroots activist Libby Frattaroli. While collecting signatures, Libby displayed a photo of a Spanish galgo—a breed similar to greyhounds—that had been killed by hanging. Greyhound breeders learned of Libby's gaffe, and never stopped claiming that our photographic evidence was obtained outside the United States. Track owner Sarkis even said in a television interview that our photographs were from France, a country with no commercial greyhound racing at all. Such was our first introduction to the unscrupulous tactics racing interests would use against us over the next two decades. Greyhound breeders and track owners were hardened by decades of political strife and viewed the process as a game in which nothing was out of bounds. Perhaps no one personified this cynicism more than Florida lobbyist Jack Cory, who would enter our story some time later.

In July 2000, we traveled to the Animal Rights conference in Washington, D.C., which was debuting again after being inactive for several years. Carey was a panel speaker, and he and Christine spent the weekend telling attendees about the Grey2k effort. We held a private lunch with movement leaders, which resulted in little tangible help but did help to boost our morale. Wayne Pacelle agreed to give some help, but only after we agreed to make changes aimed at increasing the odds of winning. To reassure Wayne, we hired longtime political adman Peter Fenn, with whom he had once collaborated on a landmark California ballot measure to protect mountain lions.

As Summer turned to Fall, the debate over Question 3 became both fiery and antagonistic. Members of the Teamsters Local 25 Union physically threatened our volunteers at public events. Track owners hired an operative from D.C. named Glenn Totten and spent millions on a slick television blitz. The first opposition ad featured a Catholic priest, named Father Guarino, in full vestments with his adopted greyhound. But this ad was only the beginning of the war of misinformation waged against Question 3. The next industry ad showcased the supposed testimonial of a former state police lieutenant, who said he had worked at a Massachusetts dog track for decades and had never seen any animal abuse. He spoke while standing next to a police cruiser. The third attack featured Colorado greyhound trainer Doris Souza with her dogs and children. She told viewers that she depended on dog racing to feed her kids. The fourth and final ad was a pure, vicious, *ad hominem* salvo, calling us radicals and liars. Vastly outspent by a margin of 5-1, we were only able to air one single ad that highlighted greyhound cruelty. The so-called Massachusetts Animal Interest Alliance, an entity formed by the track owners themselves, also ran print advertisements to scare voters. One ad led with the headline "BEWARE," and claimed that "if you eat meat, drink milk, wear leather and enjoy hunting or fishing then your rights are in jeopardy!" This particular design also included a caricature of an animal rights activist holding a sign reading "Rescue the Rats."

Our opponents also made objectively false claims about the treatment of greyhounds in Massachusetts. For example, its literature stated that there had "never been a documented case of abuse at a Massachusetts racing facility in 65 years of operation." In reality, nine emaciated and injured greyhounds had been abandoned at a Raynham farm only months earlier by a man who had recently been licensed as an assistant greyhound trainer and owner. This was only the latest in a long line of greyhound welfare scandals in the state. More than a hundred greyhounds had died in a series of fires at the so-called "Lynn kennel compound," where the Wonderland dogs were held. Additionally, racing greyhounds had been routinely abandoned and killed at animal shelters in Brockton and Pittsfield for decades. Between 1996 and 1999, a total of two hundred and eighty greyhounds had been destroyed or died of racing injuries at Wonderland and at Raynham Park. Industry defenders ignored these problems altogether, perhaps trying to convince themselves that they did not exist.

Then, a few days before the election, Charlie Sarkis filed a $10 million defamation claim against Christine, Carey, David, and Dr. Jill. This was a classic "shoot the messenger" strategy. Sarkis had become infuriated when he learned we had used a news clip of him in our campaign: dressed in one of his dramatic suits, he shook his head and insisted that dogs "were not abused, not killed" at his track. Now, he wanted payback because he looked ridiculous! He demanded not just financial damages but also the immediate take-down of our television ads. Learning of this, stations began removing us from their cycle, and only restored the ads after receiving a legal memo from Christine and our outside counsel. Christine will never forget the day she walked into the old basement office and Carey barked at her, "They are taking our ads down, you need to get them back up tonight." Was Carey trying to scare Christine, or did he just have exceptional confidence in her? It is hard to say, even now.

Sarkis' legal gambit was widely covered in the *Boston Globe* and other media outlets, undoubtedly scaring many voters away. Sarkis could never have imagined that this dirty trick would later turn out to be a blessing for the greyhounds. His lawsuit forced all of us on the Grey2k Committee to stay together and keep working, even after the election, if only to defend ourselves. This led to the continuation of our work for the greyhounds, long after we would have normally shut down.

As election day approached, it was clear that the result would be razor thin. In fact, if Question 3 had been voted on the day before or the day after the election, it's possible the greyhounds would have won. But on Tuesday, November 7, the Massachusetts Greyhound Protection Act was rejected by the narrowest of margins, 51% to 49%. This loss was one of the closest ballot question results in state history, and left us utterly devastated.

CHAPTER 5

A HIDDEN MAP

"If you know the enemy and know yourself, you need not fear the result of a hundred battles."

—Sun Tzu

The defeat of Question 3 left Christine and Carey heartbroken. Naively, Christine had truly believed that the greyhounds would win—if only because it had been so hard to collect the signatures, to secure a place on the ballot, to raise funds and educate the public, and most especially because we were *right*. But Carey had feared for the worst. As for the volunteers across the state, they were sad and angry because they knew the dogs would pay with their lives for our human failure. Innocent hounds would continue to die at Wonderland and Raynham, with no end in sight. All of our hard work seemed to have been for naught. Meanwhile, our opponents were far from gracious winners. After the election, we received an invitational postcard offering free admission to come to the Raynham Park victory celebration. The message was addressed to "GreyKKK." There was also a great deal of backbiting and finger-pointing within our own camp. The Grey2K steering committee members had become deeply invested in a successful outcome and were in shock. Looking for someone to blame, one committee member told Carey that it was well past time for him to go back to Oregon.

Still, with each passing day, a new dream began to grow. We came to appreciate that little Grey2K had gone toe-to-toe with a politically powerful animal abuse industry, fought hard on pure animal welfare grounds, and nearly won! This awakening gave us hope and provided the motivation we needed to keep fighting. We reflected deeply on every aspect of our strategy, asking ourselves what had worked and what had not. With the benefit of hindsight, it was clear that the initial strategy from Doug Rubin had been absolutely on target. We had failed to show voters what life was like for racing greyhounds in Massachusetts. Furthermore, we had not raised enough money to deliver our message. Although it was painful to face these hard truths, doing so was the only real way to move forward.

Years later, we now see that fickle fate takes a path of its own choosing. Had we prevailed with the first Question 3 vote, a national organization never would have formed, and our journey would have ended years ago. We have learned that sometimes, victory is defeat. Conversely, a loss can actually be the basis for greater success in the future. In our case, the failure of Question 3 laid the foundation for a movement to end greyhound racing in the United States. We imagined a nationwide campaign to end greyhound racing, reasoning that the dogs in West Virginia were suffering just as much as the dogs in Massachusetts and in all the other states with operating tracks. We knew that such an endeavor would take many years and require an infrastructure that was capable of winning political battles, including ballot questions. Thankfully, we had one powerful asset to start with: the realization that we didn't know what we were doing! This may seem paradoxical, but through embracing our inexperience, we found freedom to experiment and give ourselves a license to make mistakes. This was absolutely essential to our growth.

Through trial and error in the years that followed, we discovered a more effective method of greyhound advocacy, one that took inspiration from many sources. From Tom Grey, we incorporated a grassroots commitment to build something bigger than ourselves.

From Wayne Pacelle, we learned that the fight for justice is inherently a political fight, and that we are obligated to master modern political tactics such as polling and legislative advocacy in order to succeed. We read extensively about the animal rights and abolition movements, gaining ideas from historical writings, including *Bury the Chains* by Adam Hochschild. From Sun Tzu, we learned that we had to acquire a deep understanding of both ourselves and our opponents. Our greatest inspiration, however, was always the struggle itself, which we came to view as a living, breathing being with its own will and desires. The fight contained within itself a hidden map that led us forward, if we were brave enough to follow it.

Our first obstacle was the Sarkis lawsuit, which was still pending when we began to reorganize. It gave us a reason to exist, and another opportunity to make history. In preparing our defense, our lawyers explained that we had been hit with a classic SLAPP suit, which stands for "strategic litigation against public participation." If we could prove that Sarkis filed his lawsuit to block us from exercising our guaranteed First Amendment rights of free speech, the claim would not only be dismissed, but Sarkis would have to pay all of our legal fees. We filed an anti-SLAPP motion, and thankfully, the court agreed. Although the wealthy track owner was able to delay the inevitable for nine long years by appealing multiple times, Sarkis eventually had to pay out $40,000 in fines and interest—money we then used to help fund our nationwide strategy to end greyhound racing.

In those early days, Carey drafted an elaborate, multi-state proposal, which argued that dog racing was a national problem and needed a national solution. We envisioned a non-profit focused on political advocacy and public education, which utilized the state legislative process, the court system, the free press, and the ballot initiative process to pass laws to protect greyhounds. We shared our proposal with luminaries in the animal protection movement and asked for personal meetings. Few offers came, but one bold person stepped up to help. Legendary animal welfare pioneer Marian Probst of Fund for Animals agreed to see us in her New York City office, listened to us carefully, and told us flat out that we would probably fail. But then she reached into her handbag, gave us a personal check for $2,000, and wished us well. This was the seed money we desperately needed to launch our new game plan. On February 7, 2001, we officially formed GREY2K USA with the money Marian donated. Our initial board included Dr. Jill Hopfenbeck, Reverend Tom Grey, Doug Rubin, Anna Piccolo of Cambridge, and longtime animal advocate Dena Jones of California.

In the beginning, Carey took on the role of President while Christine served as Vice President. This was a reflection on the fact that Christine would be going to law school four nights a week, and it was thought that Carey would have to shoulder the operational load. Unfortunately, our titles gave others the impression that we were not equals, a presumption that Christine fought against for many years. The most galling disrespect occurred when callers would mistake her as Carey's personal secretary. (For the record, Carey is one of the fastest typists going, and Christine pecks away). Leaders of other animal protection groups would regularly contact the office and ask for Carey's legal opinion. This was the last straw for Christine! She had been raised to believe that her hard work and drive meant she would succeed (or fail) on her own terms. She had never considered taking a second seat to anyone. This troublesome dynamic would change in 2005, at least internally. Without telling Christine, Carey decided to step down from the Board of Directors. At our annual meeting, held at Café Marliave on Beacon Hill, he presented her with a golden greyhound, congratulated her on graduating from law school, and nominated her as the new President of GREY2K USA—a position she has held ever since. More than a gesture, this was Carey's way of showing Christine that she was valued.

In July of 2001, we were again drawn into a legal dispute with Sarkis, but this time as spectators. Several disappointed volunteers had rallied around an erratic activist named Kitty Granquist. Kitty had been formally removed from Grey2K a year earlier, due to her disruptive behavior. Nevertheless, she had managed to attract followers, and began organizing protests outside restaurants owned by Charlie Sarkis: the Back Bay Restaurant Group, Abe & Louies, Paparazzi, and other high end dining establishments. At one of her events, Kitty kicked a seventy-two-year-old security guard in the groin. Sarkis knew that we had nothing to do with her but used the proceedings to draw us into the controversy, to depose and harass us. Straight out of central casting, Sarkis' lawyer Kevin Considine had the air of a consigliere. Carey was interviewed first, and on the advice of civil rights attorney Gretchen Van Ness, answered questions honestly but succinctly. When Christine was deposed, however, she decided to have some fun with the sham proceeding. When asked if she were a member of any organized group, she replied in the affirmative. Considine demanded to know the names of these groups. Christine smiled and said she was a longstanding and proud member of the Johnny Mathis Fan Club! When asked if she was a member of any other organization, Christine enthusiastically replied that she was also a member of the Pat Benatar Fan Club. Sarkis' counsel then unveiled what he thought would be a devastating blow, asking Christine under oath if she had ever heard of the Animal Liberation Front. Christine looked him straight in the eyes, placed a copy of Mario Puzo's *Godfather* on the table, and said that yes, she had absolutely heard of the ALF. It was, she told him, "just like the mafia. Everyone knows it exists, even if you can't prove it." There were no further questions.

As soon as the November election passed, Sarkis and Carney shamelessly turned their attention to the state legislature, where they sought a $5 million annual tax break. On Beacon Hill, powerful political bosses held an iron grip on the process, marginalizing individual lawmakers and outsiders. We knew we could not win on the merits and, just as our initial bills had failed in years gone by, we would not succeed in defeating the track owners' legislation. As a result, we were forced to adopt an indirect strategy. We continued to oppose the bill, but privately began to lobby for the inclusion of animal welfare reforms. We found a champion in progressive Representative Pat Jehlen from Somerville. Jehlen filed multiple amendments to the tax break bill, one to require that tracks publicly disclose injuries and report on the fate of dogs that finish racing, another to prohibit racing on days of extreme heat and cold, and a third to create a state greyhound adoption trust fund supported by a percentage of every live race bet. After a tough fight and a nerve-racking floor debate, Jehlen, fellow Democrat Cheryl Rivera, and Republican Reed Hillman, won passage of the recordkeeping provision and the adoption trust fund, but were unable to pass the extreme weather prohibition.

The approval of these reforms was an important lesson for us. We learned that passing legislation is very different from the initiative process. While ballot questions force an up or down vote, the legislative process is designed to produce compromise. Track owners were so focused on their tax break that they failed to understand the risk that injury and death reporting presented. With the benefit of hindsight, it's clear that this transparency measure was a breakthrough in our fight to end greyhound racing. But in those early days, Christine stood alone in pushing it as a strategy. Most importantly, this first legislative victory taught us that our job was to act as representatives for the dogs. It wasn't our mission to make decisions based on what we would like to happen, but instead to get as much benefit for the dogs as possible from each situation. Sometimes that meant extracting concessions in an industry bill, while other times it necessitated defeating bad legislation altogether. We had an obligation to be practical, stay true to our mission, and to look for opportunities wherever they could be found. We also had to face the fact that we weren't going to win every fight, but that we *must* keep trying. The value of perseverance would later be reinforced by our battles in New Hampshire and other states, where we came to realize that small, incremental advance can lead to ultimate victory.

The year 2002 marked the start of a long fight against the legalization of slot machines at dog tracks in several states, including Massachusetts, New Hampshire, Alabama, Arizona, Colorado, and Florida. We weren't broadly against these measures, but instead opposed provisions designed to create new state mandates for dog racing, which required a percentage of the new gambling profits be set aside and used to subsidize purses—the prizes given to kennels with winning dogs. During these battles, we forged a close relationship with the anti-gambling community. This was a partnership based on mutual interests, although Christine and Carey were also personally opposed to commercial gambling. In March of 2002, Carey joined the Board of Directors of Tom Grey's National Coalition Against Legalized Gambling, which later became Stop Predatory Gambling.

GREY2K USA volunteers rally against dog track slot machines on the steps of the Massachusetts State House, April 5, 2006 (Suzanne Kreiter/Boston Globe)

Arizona became an early flash point in this gambling fight, after racetracks in the Grand Canyon State succeeded in placing Proposition 201 to legalize slots at tracks before voters. Not only would the existing tracks have access to untold wealth if the measure passed, but several long-closed venues like Yuma Greyhound Park and Black Canyon would reopen to get a piece of the action. After reaching out to possible allies, Christine received a handwritten letter from a woman in Phoenix. She warned, "The people controlling the race tracks here, and probably elsewhere, are very dangerous. My husband served on the Arizona Racing Commission for six years and was threatened with his life. I learned a great deal and it was all traumatic for me, but the really dangerous part is what concerns me for anyone trying to stop this awful 'sport.' I would like to do whatever I can to work with you, but quite frankly, I am afraid." Another friend sent a more encouraging card depicting a child hugging a greyhound and wrote, "Here in Tucson, everyone is looking forward to November 5th to witness the defeat of the abusers. I am including photos of our rally!"

That Summer, we launched a strong opposition campaign, using the simple message that greyhound cruelty shouldn't be rewarded. Working with Stephanie Nichols-Young of the Animal Legal Defense Fund and $17,000 in funding plus goodwill assistance from groups such as Best Friends, Last Chance for Animals, the Doris Day Animal League, the American Society for the Prevention of Cruelty to Animals, the Humane Society of the United States, and Friends of Animals, our get-out-the-vote radio blitz hit the airwaves. Meanwhile, seventeen local Native American tribes in Arizona also opposed Prop 201 and released a TV ad mocking "Arizona Joe," the folksy actor the tracks had hired to direct voters to "just do the math and vote yes." Meanwhile, the "Yes on Prop 201" folks took great pains to distance themselves from the fact that the measure would prop up dog racing. Instead, gambling interests emphasized their promise to provide $300 million annually for education, senior health care, and deficit reduction, and to "control gambling." In November, voters proved they had seen through the rhetoric and firmly rejected the placement of slots at tracks by an 80% to 20% margin. The power of working in a coalition had been the key to our success. We were thrilled, and very relieved, by this outcome.

That same year, the public received another reminder of the fate of unprofitable greyhounds when the *New York Times* broke the grim story of Robert Rhodes. Rhodes was working as a security guard at the Pensacola Greyhound Track when he was arrested and charged with felony animal cruelty. According to the *Times*, he had taken thousands of unwanted dogs from the track over the years, charging $10 apiece to shoot them in the head and bury them in mass graves on his Alabama property. The local District Attorney David Whetstone was horrified by the smell of death and piles of dead bodies found there, calling the farm a veritable "Dachau for dogs." Rhodes died before trial and none of his co-conspirators, including NGA favorite Ursula O'Donnell, were ever brought to justice. In stomach-churning fashion, Rhodes expressed no remorse and even told officials that he was doing the dogs a favor. When he had first entered the business more than fifty years earlier, unwanted dogs were set loose in a field to run and be used as target practice. By contrast, he offered a "quick, clean death." Sadly, the bodies of dogs who had been shot in the snout, the neck, or the jaw told a different story.

It was also at this time that we were to encounter our first major pro-industry huckster. Ron Hevener was a Mae West impersonator and a self-described "accomplished artist who started out by selling handmade souvenirs and telling stories to tourists at Pennsylvania Dutch farmers' markets." He formed the Greyhound Racing Association of America in March 2002, promising to use his media

Dead greyhounds found buried on the property of
Robert Rhodes in Alabama, 2002 (State of Florida)

talents to expose "animal rights corporations" and spread a positive message about dog racing and other animal-related industries. Within a month, one hundred greyhound breeders had paid their dues to become members of the GRAA. In the end, Hevener's main "accomplishment" was to delay the full enforcement of our Massachusetts adoption trust fund and to disrupt the Greyhound Care and Adoption Council created to implement it. Years later, Hevener was charged with starving twenty-nine of his horses and indicted on five counts of animal cruelty. He quietly disappeared from the racing debate, although he still sells greyhound figurines today and advertises himself as an animal lover.

Following our initial legislative struggle in Massachusetts, we began to expand our lobbying reach. In Florida, we retained well-known Democratic attorney Mark Herron, who tracked pending legislation and performed legal research, helping us to find new ways to attack the industry. We renewed our coalition strategy and gratefully accepted the financial support and advice we received from the Greyhound Protection League, the Ark Trust, the National Greyhound Adoption Program, and the National Coalition Against Gambling Expansion, to name just a few. Together, we had the resources to go to court and help block an early attempt to prop up Florida's then-seventeen dog tracks with slot machines. A year later, we hired an up-and-coming Republican lobbyist named Marc Reichelderfer, who would serve as a lodestar for our Florida fight over the next twenty years. Marc was quiet, modest, family-oriented, and effective. He knew everyone and was universally liked and respected. Years later, Carey snuck Marc into a local kennel compound so that he could see for himself how racing greyhounds lived. Marc was horrified and left with an even greater commitment to ending greyhound racing.

It was with Marc's help that our coalition was able to stop legislation that would have subsidized dog tracks with increased poker profits. Brought forward in the state legislature by then-state Senator Debbie Wasserman Schultz and featuring a requirement for tracks to open adoption booths, it also provided new revenue to the tracks, causing more harm than good. We circulated action alert postcards and placed a full page, open letter to Governor Jeb Bush in the *Tallahassee Democrat*. Meanwhile, newspapers had begun reporting on the major injuries and deaths of racing dogs even as the story of Robert Rhodes continued to cast its long shadow on the industry. On May 27, 2002, Governor Bush vetoed the Trojan Horse bill.

In early 2004, we obtained records that greyhounds were testing positive for cocaine at tracks across Florida. Christine sought the help of then-Attorney General Charlie Crist and also wrote to every state attorney asking for intervention. They all refused to act. Then in July, we responded to calls from local advocates and joined an effort that succeeded in stopping Independence Day fireworks at the Bonita dog track, something which caused panic and stress for area greyhounds each year. But this local victory was immediately followed by the news that South Florida racetracks were bringing a constitutional amendment before voters in an attempt to authorize thousands of slot machines at the Flagler and Hollywood dog tracks. As we began to organize a "No on Amendment 4" message, we were called to a secret meeting in Washington D.C. with Florida dog track interests. Waiting for us were track promoter Danny Adkins, pollster Bob Meadows, and Fred Havenick, the former President of the American Greyhound Track Operators Association. Havenick had appeared in the 1993 National Geographic exposé and expressed regret at that time for the industry's poor humane record. During our encounter he spoke passionately about wanting to transition away from racing and appeared to sincerely care about the greyhounds. By contrast, Adkins reminded us of Charlie Sarkis. He gave the impression of being a cold-blooded man who cared only for the buck and not the bark. He threatened to "run dogs into the ground" if we refused to cooperate and support his slots amendment. There was even a hint of some reward for our acquiescence. Both Havenick and Adkins argued that expanded gambling could allow them to transition away from racing—but only if we endorsed them with the voters. After listening to this "offer," Christine and Carey refused to capitulate, and left the meeting more determined than ever to fight the corrupt racetracks.

Our attorney, Mark Herron, filed a lawsuit against Amendment 4, arguing that it had reached the ballot by using the signatures of dead people to qualify. The Florida Supreme Court rejected the challenge as speculative and most importantly not ripe, finding that no harm had been done since no vote had yet been taken. Undeterred, we reached out to allies and assembled a hodgepodge coalition of animal protection groups, competing commercial interests, and anti-gambling activists to fight the question. They published articles in their newsletters and on their websites. They also chipped in funds for full page newspaper ads featuring our board member's dog Gracie imploring voters, "Don't Reward Cruelty, Vote NO on 4." Our closest partner was No Casinos, led by John Sowinski. Sowinski had passed several ballot questions, and previously worked on constitutional amendments to ban the use of drag nets in state waters and outlaw the intense confinement of pigs on factory farms. We barnstormed the state, addressing editorial boards and meeting with local volunteers in Tallahassee, Jacksonville, Orlando, St. Petersburg, Miami, and Naples. Volunteers handed out thousands of flyers at public events across the state, targeting presidential campaign rallies in particular. Animal advocates flooded their local papers with letters-to-the-editor for the greyhounds. There were several coordinators around the state, but a longtime People for the Ethical Treatment of Animals supporter named Kathy Pelton really stood out. She created gift bags with flyers and bumper stickers that she hung on the doors of thousands of homes in the Miami area alone. Her leadership was phenomenal. Meanwhile, the racetracks spent millions on television ads that promised a huge pay off for schools from slot machine proceeds. Jim Horne, a former Education Commissioner was one of the champions of this misleading claim.

All our hard work paid off on election night when the tracks ended up losing. But alas, our victory was short-lived. In a matter of days, additional votes were miraculously discovered in South Florida, which tipped the balance in favor of the racetrack proposal. We made one last attempt to scuttle Amendment 4 by renewing our lawsuit based on submission of thousands of fraudulent signatures but were eventually forced to withdraw due to lack of resources.

As would happen many times, this setback was quickly followed by an unexpected victory, this time at the far end of the country. On Christmas Eve, 2004, Multnomah Greyhound Park in Oregon closed forever. This was a particularly demoralizing event for the industry, as Multnomah had been a flagship racing venue for decades. It also meant that dog racing was over in the entire Pacific Northwest. When the track was finally razed, Christine made sure to share the demolition video with advocates across the country. Years later, she was to learn how devastated the greyhound racing world had been at this loss. It seemed that at least some greyhound breeders had begun to see the handwriting on the wall.

As our work continued and we sought out new opportunities for the greyhounds, office conditions were becoming unbearable. The GREY2K USA headquarters in Davis Square, Somerville was very humble, and that was fine with us. But after the 2000 election, the one-room space was starting to become inadequate. A sign on the door read "Suite B9" but this closet-sized room was actually a disused utility nook in a basement room, two floors below the offices of CEASE. Evelyn Kimber had convinced the landlord to let us move in and had even gifted us a worktable and several filing cabinets, all of which Christine uses to this day. There was no heat but, on the bright side, it was very cool in the summer. The one major problem was that we sat below water level and experienced regular office floods. One Winter, we had to move all the computers off the floor, and everyone took to wearing galoshes to keep their feet dry. Space heaters had to be turned off to avoid electrical fires, so the office was both cold and wet. When green and black mold appeared on the walls, and another tenant happened to vacate a larger office space on higher ground, we moved fast! Years later, the flooding reached even this second office and we had to leave the building altogether.

In 2004, the Florida fight shifted to the legislature, where lawmakers were required to pass implementation legislation for the racetracks' slot machine bill. At the recommendation of Marc Reichelderfer, we retained a large team of lobbyists led by Mac Stipanovich. A longtime veteran of the Tallahassee lobby corps, Stipanovich had served as a key strategist for George W. Bush.

He was ingenious and highly regarded by his peers. He was also an independent thinker and would later be a key figure in the #NeverTrump movement. We tasked Stipanovich and his team with three goals: to prevent any legal requirement that greyhound racing continue in order to operate slot machines, to defeat all attempts to create dog racing subsidies from slot machine profits, and to pass a mandate for greyhound injury reporting.

As the session ticked down to *sine die* adjournment, it appeared we would succeed on two of these three points. Although the legislature had unfortunately adopted a racing requirement, we had defeated all subsidy provisions and were poised to win on injury reporting. However, on the last night of the session, the bill collapsed under its own weight as competing track owners engaged in a last-minute internecine fight for more tax breaks. The legislature would come back months later to again pass an implementation bill, but this time, greyhound record-keeping was left off the table.

Meanwhile, local votes were held to give final approval for slots at dog tracks in Miami-Dade and Broward Counties. The local referendum passed in Broward, but failed in Dade. The Havenick family brought the issue back before Miami voters again in 2006 and won. With that vote, the years-long fight over slot machines at South Florida dog tracks ended. Christine crashed the victory party at the Miami dog track and spoke with reporters about the terrible impact the Amendment would have on dogs. Mrs. Havenick and her sons did not appreciate her presence, to say the least, and they had Christine physically carried off the premises, depositing her outside in the parking lot. Not to be outdone, she continued her interviews in the comfort of the TV sound trucks outside. This was not the first time, and would certainly not be the last time, that Christine would be kicked out of a racetrack!

The slot machine fight challenged us in our home state of Massachusetts as well. Thankfully, we managed to defeat these "racino" (racetrack casino) bills for several years in a row. If we had lost just once, greyhound racing would have become even further entrenched, and history may have turned out quite differently. During these formative years, we found ourselves looking for major victories but often coming up short. We scrambled to pass any small reform we could, while the organization remained underfunded, discounted by other groups, and lacking in volunteer support. But then we were called to the most important debate of our early years. And it all started in New Hampshire, with a dog named Fiery Elegance.

Chapter 6

A Simple Choice

"The abuse has been going on for so many years and they figured they were untouchable . . . please hurry before more die."

—New Hampshire kennel worker

On a warm summer evening in July 1998, an accountant named Mike Trombley was serving as a temporary racetrack official at The Lodge at Belmont, a ramshackle dog track located in the Lakes Region of New Hampshire. During the first race, a black greyhound named Fiery Elegance stumbled as she came out of the turn, having just suffered a broken leg. Moments later, the injured dog was taken to a building behind the track and away from the public eye. When the young trainer responsible for Fiery Elegance was told she had a broken leg, he immediately asked that she be destroyed.

"Fiery Elegance was the first dog to die in my presence," Mike would later say. "I held her as she took her last breath." A few days later, he looked up the state gambling data for Fiery Elegance, did the math, and realized that New Hampshire was going to receive one measly dollar in revenue for the race in which she had died. This experience had a profound impact on Mike, but only found an outlet a few years later when he happened to learn about the Greyhound Protection League. Mike reached out after hearing a radio interview and was put in contact with veterinarian Jill Hopfenbeck. Through Jill, he met Carey and Christine, and the four of us collaborated on a Fox TV report about the killing and mass burial of unprofitable greyhounds behind New Hampshire tracks. Mike eventually joined the GREY2K USA Board, where he would soon be followed by another Granite Stater, Paul LaFlamme.

In March of 2002, while we were still finding our footing, we had sent an introductory letter about greyhound racing to every lawmaker in states with a dog track. We received only a handful of responses, but the one from Paul made the entire exercise worthwhile. The owner of his own real estate firm, Paul came from a well-known family in Nashua and was the celebrated leader of the Spartans, a championship youth drum and bugle team. He had just been elected to office and was serving his first term in the State House of Representatives. Paul was moved by what he learned about the treatment of greyhounds and agreed to champion an injury reporting bill.

In January of 2003, Christine wrote and Paul filed the first ever standalone legislation to require the public reporting of greyhound racing injuries in the United States. Although HB 520 was straightforward and represented little cost to the industry, the racetracks and their well-connected lobbyists vigorously opposed it. Because of their obstruction, when the bill was heard in the House Committee on Environment and Agriculture, Committee members chose to "retain" the proposal for further study, meaning it would not be voted on for another year. In January 2004, the Committee took up Paul's bill once more, with the intention of killing it. On a 12 to 5 vote, the measure was deemed "ITL" which stands for "inexpedient to legislate." In the normal course of events, this would have been a death knell. However, there was still a glimmer of hope for the greyhounds. Unlike in other states, a New Hampshire committee cannot block legislation from a full hearing in the House or Senate. The Granite State legislature is unique in that all bills ultimately receive a full vote among all lawmakers in their originating chamber. That said, all bills leave committee with an official recommendation that is almost always respected. Lawmakers have the right to contest committee decisions, but rarely do. A majority vote is needed for an override, so this maneuver is rarely attempted. But we decided to give it a try!

As a freshman who had never before spoken on the floor, Paul was hardly the ideal candidate to challenge custom. Nonetheless, we launched a major lobbying effort to do just that. GREY2K USA board members and staff, along with the Humane Society of the United States, personally called all four hundred Representatives. Lawmakers in New Hampshire do not have professional staff or offices, so we phoned them at their homes. We kept a running vote count of the chamber and spent weeks pleading, cajoling, and appealing to members for their support.

When the bill was finally called up for debate, Paul was ready to make history. In his maiden speech, he spoke passionately and logically about the need for increased oversight of the racing industry. He pointed out that if dog track claims about low injury and death rates were true, then they had nothing to hide. In fact, his bill would actually prove their position. Most of all, Paul said he really didn't know how many dogs were being hurt at New Hampshire racetracks, or whether things were as bad as some feared, and he wanted the opportunity to find out. His commonsense approach spoke volumes. Over the next hour, what had been a lopsided committee motion to defeat the injury reporting bill was transformed into a heated argument on the House floor. As yet more speakers rose, Paul found support from several unexpected allies, including an odd, combustible man named Steve Vaillancourt. Vaillancourt would later play a starring role in the greyhound debate, but these were early days. As Paul made his closing argument, it became clear that he had a serious chance of defeating the ITL recommendation. His final words came from the heart, as he pleaded with his colleagues to "please, vote for the dogs."

Time seemed to slow down as the debate ended and the Speaker of the House opened the voting machines. A heavy tension fell over the room, and we desperately tried to count whether there were more red or more green dots appearing on the big boards on each side of the chamber. With a loud buzz, voting ended, and the result flashed up on the screen. 166 Representatives had voted to kill the greyhound bill, and 168 had voted to revive it. Paul had done it! By a mere two-vote margin, he had overturned the Environment and Agriculture Committee and its powerful Chair. Wasting no time, he jumped up to the podium again and made the parliamentary motion that his bill "ought to pass." HB 520 was then adopted with little debate, and even picked up another eighteen votes when all was said and done. To say we were shocked would be an understatement. HB 520 marked one of first times in American history that the greyhound industry had flexed its muscle against a reform bill brought by animal advocates and suffered defeat. We had been given yet another taste of how change sometimes happens in the most unexpected ways.

After this dramatic victory, Paul's injury reporting bill was advanced to the Senate Ways and Means Committee. Despite our best efforts, the bill received another ITL recommendation, this time on a unanimous 5-0 vote. Overturning a unanimous vote seemed utterly inconceivable, but we had nothing to lose. Lightning couldn't strike twice for the dogs, could it?

Attempting to revive a bill in the New Hampshire Senate is a fundamentally different challenge than it is in the House. As mentioned, there are four hundred House members, making it the largest continuously standing representative body in the world. By contrast, the Senate has only twenty-four members, and leadership keeps a very tight grip on each and every one of them. Thankfully, we had the Dean of the Senate, Sheila Roberge of Bedford, on our side. A staunch conservative blessed with elegance and style, Senator

Roberge had first become involved in politics during the Ronald Reagan era. All told, she served in the Senate for more than a quarter century. She was respected and held in high esteem by virtually everyone. Her first passion was fighting for animals, and when Paul reached out to ask for her help, she readily agreed. It didn't hurt that he had just been named "Young Republican of the Year!"

Senator Roberge was second to none as a vote counter. She possessed an intuitive ability to listen and identify opportunities to pick up support. "If a Senator looks me in the eye, shakes my hand, and tells me I have her vote, then she is a yes," Roberge explained to us. "Otherwise, she is a no and I have more work to do." Roberge worked on her colleagues for three straight days, undoubtedly making a few trades and private deals along the way. She also successfully enlisted the help of a powerful colleague, Ted Gatsas, who would become Senate President two years later. When the bill came up for a vote, Roberge earned a strong 14-9 victory for the dogs. Like the little engine that could, House Bill 520 had miraculously passed the State Legislature and was transmitted to the governor for signature. We soon learned, however, that our work was not yet finished.

Exactly two months after the Senate passed the greyhound injury reporting bill, dog track lobbyists convinced Governor Craig Benson to reject the measure. His veto message was a clear sign of how threatened the industry felt about disclosing information concerning the fate of dogs racing in the state. Republican Governor Benson cited increased state expenditures, decried what he viewed as unfair penalties for falsifying injury reports, and claimed the industry was already "subject to enough regulation as it is." His greatest concern, however, was the beginning of a real discussion about the cruelty of dog racing. "Many supporters of the bill seek to put an end to greyhound racing in New Hampshire," the Governor wrote. "We should be concerned about the potential loss of jobs associated with the closing down of the state's greyhound industry."

New Hampshire State Senator Sheila Roberge, June 14, 2010
(AP Photo/Jim Cole, © 2010 AP)

His rejection was a blow for us, but we had fought too hard to give up now, and there was still one final option left. Dog advocates needed to convince lawmakers to set aside the Governor's veto. A two-thirds majority vote in both chambers would be required, meaning that we would have to retain all of our "yes" votes and turn scores of "no" votes to our side. Fortunately for the greyhounds, Governor Benson was unpopular, even with members of his own party. The greyhounds definitely had an opening.

One month later, after receiving thousands of phone calls, letters, and personal pleas, the House voted to override Governor Benson's veto with an overwhelming 290-52 vote. Hours later, the Senate also voted to override the veto by a margin of 18-6. We had won our first major legislative victory against powerful dog track owners. This miraculous outcome was a sign that our fight was indeed worthwhile and that we could win against great odds. This initial success also marked the beginning of an annual legislative fight for the greyhounds in New Hampshire, a process that continued for many years and taught us the need for patience and determination.

As we prepared for the next legislative session, which would commence in early 2005, the New Hampshire dog tracks became embroiled in several high-profile controversies. In late 2004, authorities received letters accusing kennel operator Robert LeClair and several of his family members of regularly destroying dogs and committing acts of physical abuse. The letters were signed with first names only, and claimed to be from track workers at Hinsdale Greyhound Park. They included a lengthy list of dogs that LeClair had allegedly killed. One letter expressed urgency and ended with the plea, "please hurry before more die." These allegations found their way to State Veterinarian Dr. Clifford McGinnis, who tried (unsuccessfully) to secure the assistance of local Police Chief Wayne Gallagher. In a letter to the Chief, an exasperated McGinnis wrote that "[I]t was very disappointing and surprising that I could not get your help on an investigation of animal cruelty at the Greyhound track." The Hinsdale Greyhound Park Board of Judges, an extension of the Pari-Mutuel Commission, also refused to take action. In dismissing the allegations, the Board found that "there may be an ulterior motive to the charges as [the accusers] compete for purse money and several of the people making the complaints were asked to leave due to Hinsdale downsizing their live racing."

In January, the general manager for The Lodge at Belmont, Richard Hart, was indicted for his involvement in a massive offshore illegal gambling conspiracy that included money laundering in association with the Gambino crime family. Hart would later plead guilty. The scandal raised doubts about the Pari-Mutuel Commission, which was charged with enforcing the integrity of racing. The PMC had allowed Hart and his two brothers to operate dog tracks for many years, despite their past convictions for illegal gambling. After a media firestorm, Belmont was shuttered and remained closed until June of 2006.

Senator Roberge capitalized on these scandals by filing a bill in the 2005 session to eliminate an annual subsidy for dog racing. Every year, $325,000 was diverted from the state's Education Trust Fund to underwrite the costs of drug testing at the state's dog tracks. The industry handout revealed the power and corruption of the racing industry and provided a platform for us to continue a broader debate on the merits of dog racing. As expected, Senator Roberge's anti-subsidy bill received a negative recommendation from its reviewing committee. But by this point, we held an irrational confidence in our ability to overturn adverse committee findings and pushed on unfazed. Unfortunately, our luck did not hold, and attempts to revive the measure failed by the razor thin margin of 11-13 that year.

Muzzled greyhound in cage at Hinsdale Greyhound Park, 2006 (Linda Miranda)

In 2006, we filed the same bill in the House, ensuring it would be considered in the lower chamber first. We did this to generate some momentum before having to face the inescapable reckoning of the Senate. Our House sponsor was the brilliant Steve Vaillancourt. We first laid eyes on Representative Vaillancourt in the Spring of 2006 when he came and sat down next to us in the public gallery of the House chamber. The New Hampshire State House is a beautiful building, with magnificent murals adorning the walls. But it lacks the gold-plated ostentation of other capitol buildings and always seemed very approachable to us. Until 2016, anyone could just walk in and go right to the governor's office. There was little to no security at all. One day, Christine was stunned to meet up with the governor himself as he was taking a lunchtime promenade along the second floor. He said hello and asked how she was, but she was too stunned to answer! This was a kind of openness and lack of pretense she had never seen on Boston's Beacon Hill.

One of our approaches in the early days involved placing print ads in major newspapers, timing them to affect positive vote outcomes. One such ad, called "A Simple Choice," depicted a sad greyhound in a racetrack cage on one side with the image of a little schoolgirl sitting at her desk on the other. We asked readers, which would you choose to fund? This message had apparently caught the attention of Representative Vaillancourt. So there we were, watching proceedings on the House floor, only to notice a poorly dressed man sitting a few seats away from us, shuffling through a large stack of wrinkled papers. On top, rested a copy of our ad. It looked like he had cut it out and glued it to a piece of cardboard. At first glance, he seemed to be a transient. Hair askew, wearing a rumpled gray suit and dirty sneakers, he appeared not to have slept or shaved for days. He seemed to be watching the proceedings, but we have now come to believe that he was actually watching us! Little did we know he was an intellectual genius and would soon become our champion.

New Hampshire State Representative Steve Vaillancourt, May 20, 2009
(AP Photo/Jim Cole, File, © 2017 The Associated Press)

Over the next several years, Carey would become good friends with
him, bonding over their shared interests in public policy and love of
debate. By contrast, Vaillancourt refused to remember Christine's
name and would always refer to her as "the lawyer." Vaillancourt
was not what one might call a "people person," but he was honest
and daring and just what the greyhounds needed.

From the start, Representative Vaillancourt's advocacy for the
dogs was acrimonious. He served on the House Ways and Means
Committee, which would be the first to consider our anti-subsidy bill.
But on the day of the hearing, Vaillancourt was loudly harangued by
racetrack lobbyists sitting at the back of the room. He viewed this as
an act of disrespect and complained to the Committee Chair. The
Chairman not only ignored Vaillancourt's pleas but then proposed
a negative recommendation aimed at killing the bill and protecting
racetrack subsidies. Vaillancourt was furious. He put out an open
letter to the Chairman, blaming him for failing to enforce decorum
and saying that "a fish rots at the head and you are the head." When
House Speaker Doug Scamman received a copy of this missive,
he publicly sanctioned Vaillancourt by removing him from the

Committee altogether! So it seemed that the old boy's network was alive and well, even in Concord, and that the battle was lost.

We felt humiliated, and we stopped fighting for the bill. We made no calls, and only tuned in to watch the floor debate as a matter of routine. And that's when magic happened. Despite having no help and no allies, Vaillancourt was determined to prevail. Once the Committee's ITL recommendation was announced on the floor, Vaillancourt rose to speak. Full of passion and righteousness, he told his fellow lawmakers about the importance of ending a dishonest and wasteful giveaway to an industry that was cruel to animals. He had been unable, he emphasized, to make his case during the Committee hearing because contemptuous lobbyists had disrespected him, and in fact, disrespected the entire House. Rather than intercede and protect the honor of a member, Vaillancourt continued, the Committee Chair had encouraged and even rewarded this disrespect. The Speaker of the House had then joined in and completely silenced him. This was not fair or honest, and was an offense to the entire chamber. Vaillancourt then began to speak at a faster pace, quoting the founding fathers with such a breadth of knowledge and wit that every legislator in the chamber, friend or foe, Democrat or Republican, held on to every word. Vaillancourt finished with a smile, satisfied that he had finally gotten to speak his mind. To our amazement, the ITL recommendation was defeated by a commanding vote of 151 to 129 that day. We never doubted Steve Vaillancourt again.

After this extraordinary vote, Vaillancourt's greyhound subsidy bill moved to the Senate where it had narrowly failed the year before. After yet another ITL committee recommendation, Senator Roberge waged a bitter floor fight and succeeded in reviving the bill once on a tied vote of 12-12. That's when our opponents panicked. Dog racing ally Senator Lou D'Allesandro offered a last-minute amendment to phase-out the payments over three years, rather than end them at once. Roberge cleverly accepted this compromise, realizing that another clear win would help us reach our true objective of ending dog racing. The measure easily passed the Senate and was later signed into law by the Democratic Governor John Lynch, paving the way for our next big move.

It was around this time that we added lobbyist Nancy Johnson to our team. Nancy was a former Democratic member of the House who cared deeply about animal welfare. During the rest of the New Hampshire struggle, Nancy was always present, fighting for the greyhounds with both persistence and passion. As soon as we started working with Nancy, we saw another big sign that the tracks were in trouble. After yet another one of their bills to legalize slot machines stalled, track lobbyists struck the slots language altogether and substituted in a reduction to the state-mandated racing days, drawing down from 100 to 50. They were ending dog racing themselves! The rationale was that if they couldn't cash in on expanded gambling, at least they could improve their bottom line by cutting some of their losses. Greyhound racing had become a drag on the overall business as costs exceeded revenues. The amended legislation passed both chambers and became law. The dog tracks immediately halved their racing schedules, giving greyhounds a bit of much-needed relief.

In November of 2006, an electoral tidal wave swept over New Hampshire. The Democrats captured control of both chambers of the legislature as well as the governorship for the first time since 1874. Change was in the air, and in January of 2007, Representative Peter Schmidt from Dover agreed to introduce our bill to completely outlaw greyhound racing. Schmidt was an older man, well-liked by fellow Democrats and passionate about helping the dogs. He was joined on the bill by several strong cosponsors, including Representative Mary Cooney from Grafton and, of course, Representative Vaillancourt. We organized a working group to fight for the bill, and began to meet regularly in the Concord law office of legendary spay/neuter activist Peter Marsh. Together, we launched a lobbying campaign that far outpaced anything we'd ever tried before. For the first time, our operation became multi-faceted and included several distinct strategies that all unfolded simultaneously.

In February, we released a white paper report on greyhound racing in the state. Thanks to the transparency bill Paul LaFlamme had passed three years earlier, we could now provide lawmakers with a more accurate picture of the animal welfare problems that persisted at Hinsdale, Seabrook, and The Lodge at Belmont. In total, 716 greyhound injuries had been reported at New Hampshire tracks over a two-year-period. 184 involved broken bones, and 160 dogs had suffered career-ending injuries, died on the track, or been destroyed. The records also highlighted the tragic fate of individual dogs. For example, a one-year-old greyhound named Amber had perished on April 22, 2006, after she ran into the racetrack rail at Seabrook, cracked her skull, and suffered what the track described as "massive brain damage." A copy of our report was sent to every lawmaker, and we were able to generate a great deal of prominent news coverage. Meanwhile, working with the University of New Hampshire Survey Center, we began tracking public support for our bill. In the first survey, a prohibition of dog racing was favored by 52% and opposed by 37%. The following year, support increased to 59%.

In the Senate, Sheila Roberge filed a separate bill to require racetracks to pay for the full cost of drug testing. Up until then, dog and horse tracks were capped in their drug testing payments, and the state was losing more than half a million dollars each year. To our disappointment, the Roberge bill was retained in committee, preventing consideration for another year. But when her language was included as a one-line amendment to the 2009 budget, the claw back was easily approved without much of a fight.

Meanwhile, in the House, Schmidt's bill to outlaw dog racing was given a March hearing. The hearing room was packed, and sharply divided. Many of our shelter allies came in support but, in a replay of the Massachusetts campaign, a man of the cloth appeared in opposition. Dressed in his clerical robe and collar, the head of a local pro-racing adoption group made a grand entrance and testified that had never seen any New Hampshire greyhounds abused. To make matters even more tense, another dog racing apologist named Rory Goree, who served as the President of the industry-funded Greyhound Pets of America group, also came to deny the cruelty of dog racing. He had flown in from Arizona in the midst of a snowstorm to oppose our measure. During his testimony, he described HB 923 as an "atomic bomb" that would "cause the death of hundreds of greyhounds." Then Rory approached each committee member with a colorful handout describing Christine's supposed past as an attorney for a clandestine group called the Animal Liberation Front. Seeing this, she immediately sidled up next to him dressed in her black pinstriped suit, introduced herself as the author of the bill, and asked if they had any questions! Lawmakers could not reconcile the soft-spoken, five-foot lady in heels with the anarchist portrayed in the flyer, and some of them even refused to take his materials. Christine learned early on that confronting a bully like Rory head-on is always the best policy. Years later, Rory would become ensnared in a huge scandal after his appointment to the Arizona Racing Commission. Writing to Governor Jan Brewer, we urged her to remove Rory from this regulatory body after he publicly harassed Christine online, mocking her for suffering a near-fatal accident, calling her a "trolley wreck" and "trash," all while making sexually suggestive remarks about her appearance. In the end, Rory was allowed to keep his job, but only after publicly apologizing.

Dozens of compassionate people testified in favor of the Schmidt bill, and we believed that we might finally earn the support of a legislative committee. Sadly, our hopes were dashed when lawmakers overwhelmingly recommended the Schmidt bill be scuttled. We took our fight to the House floor where, despite our hard work, we were unable to overcome the ITL obstacle. By a final count of 198 to 138, the House voted to allow greyhound racing to continue.

Looking back, the defeat of the Schmidt bill was the end of the first stage of our work. We had found our footing, and we began to develop a methodology to bring about just outcomes, but we still weren't fully capable of overcoming all obstacles. Carey and our lobbyist Nancy had kept detailed vote count sheets, and our wonderful board member Denise McFadden had designed a stunning full-page print ad, introducing our new slogan and website: VoteForTheDogs.org. Christine organized phone calls, letters, and personal visits to all 424 lawmakers from constituents, and we received full-throttled endorsements from humane groups across the state. All of these well-intentioned and careful strategies were not to be rewarded just yet, however.

It seemed that once again, the right path for the greyhounds would be uneven. Come what may, we believed we had to "stay on the field" and keep to our posts, as Tom Grey often counseled. The next step required us to return home to Massachusetts, where a renewed battle awaited.

CHAPTER 7

RUN FOR THE ROSES

"Our greyhound's name is Hope. We didn't give her that name; she came with it. In my more fanciful moments, I almost take that for a sign."

—Paula Blanchard

The Massachusetts law that allows ballot initiatives is as arduous as it is quirky. One odd detail is that issues can only be brought back to voters after the passage of three legislative sessions, or every six years. So it would not be until 2006 that we would again have the opportunity to bring a racing ban before the citizens of our home state.

As individuals and as an organization, we had matured in the intervening years, and now managed to raise a few hundred thousand dollars per year. We also maintained a small staff and, most notably, Christine was now an attorney. For four years, Christine had worked full-time at GREY2K USA by day and attended classes in Boston at the New England School of Law by night. She was a dedicated student and worked hard, studying twelve hours a day on Saturdays and Sundays to make up for her inability to do so during the week. One night, in her third year, she noticed that the largest lecture hall at NESL was called the Carney Room. It didn't take her long to figure out that it was named after dog track owner George Carney. It turned out that he was the only non-attorney member of the school's board of trustees and personally funded all of the academic scholarships—including the one that Christine had received. As the official "New England Scholar" of the 2005 Class, her annual tuition was fully covered. Did George know he was her benefactor? Christine decided not to take any chances and kept quiet about the whole thing.

The situation came to a head the night before graduation, however, when we ran into George at the reception for Juris Doctor recipients. He spotted Christine and Carey and made a beeline for their cocktail table. He seemed a bit surprised, but pulled up a seat. Pleasantries were exchanged and we all talked a bit about our upbringing. But then, George wanted to know why we were there. Christine told him she was graduating at the top of her night school class. What firm was she joining, George asked? Smiling broadly, Christine let him know that she would not be going to any firm at all. She intended to be a lawyer for the greyhounds and would spend the next few months writing a new ballot question to end dog racing in Massachusetts. George laughed heartily and, with a devilish grin, wished us luck. He bragged that he was about to expand his operations with slot machines and that any attempt to stop him would be futile. Christine decided that this was the ideal moment to reveal the secret of her scholarship, and sincerely thanked George for sending her to law school. To his credit, Carney barely paused. He immediately insisted that he would personally present Christine with her diploma the next day. As a result, Christine's graduation photo shows herself with a beaming George Carney on stage at the Wang Theatre—all to the horror of her mother, family, and friends.

With her JD in hand, Christine kept her word and drafted a new ballot question. We began to assemble a coalition, and Wayne Pacelle argued that if we were going to go through the gargantuan effort of another signature drive, we should aim to help as many dogs as possible at once. So Christine redrafted our simple greyhound racing ban into a more generic "Dog Protection Act" that would phase out commercial dog racing, strengthen laws against dogfighting, and increase penalties for harming service dogs. Over the course of the next year, we held grassroots meetings all across the state, and with a monumental volunteer investment, successfully scaled the signature gathering mountain once again. We were ready to take our case to the people, but first faced a legal challenge brought by old man Carney. In Massachusetts, citizens' initiatives are permitted to contain multiple subjects as long as they are all reasonably related. We believed the Dog Protection Act met this test, because what could be more related than three policies designed to help dogs? Carney's lawyers argued that greyhound racing was unrelated to other dog protection measures because greyhounds are racing machines, not dogs. We saw Carney at a Supreme Court hearing, red-faced and livid. It was clear that he thought he was going to lose, and the fact that Christine had lived up to her promise was just too much for him to bear. After the proceedings, and once outside the courtroom, George very loudly growled at Christine that he wanted his money back!

But weeks later, and in a surprise ruling, the Massachusetts Supreme Judicial Court did indeed strike our proposed question from the ballot, finding that a phase-out of greyhound racing was a commercial issue and was not sufficiently related to the other two humane issues. We were gutted. It was inconceivable that thousands of dogs would continue to die because we had failed again. To this day, we believe the Dog Protection Act was constitutional and contained important reforms that were germane and which voters deserved to hear. While speaking with Assistant Attorney General Peter Sacks after the ruling, Christine came to understand that if we had offered the three-part question first, we would likely have survived review. But the fact that the other humane provisions seemed to be "added on" may have appeared like log rolling, a tactic in which non-controversial issues are inserted to pad more challenging ones. It was all about timing, he said. Whatever the reason, the greyhounds were left at the altar once more.

At the same time, GREY2K USA itself faced an existential crisis. We had focused so completely on the 2006 Massachusetts effort that all work to develop the organization had been set aside. We had bled our list, asking anyone who cared to please give like there was no tomorrow. But then "tomorrow" did come, and we had to face the music. It was sink or swim all over again. We couldn't pay our bills and faced the very real possibility of insolvency. We made emergency spending cuts and curtailed operations as best we could. It's extremely difficult to create a national non-profit without an initial seed grant or endowment, and we had begun with neither. We only had ourselves and the belief that if we didn't push forward, dog racing would go on for decades to come. As our board member Kevin Neuman liked to say, "If not you, who?" In hindsight, it's miraculous that we were able to establish ourselves at all. It was a stroke of good luck that our 2006 crash turned out to be only a close call, and that GREY2K USA managed to keep going.

Even in the midst of our disappointment and heavy financial woes, we realized we had to keep working. There was no time to sit back and feel sorry for ourselves. Within an hour of getting news of the court loss, Carey began drafting a press release and Christine set about rewriting the question. This time, it would be a ballot question to end greyhound racing only. Our grassroots allies were growing weary of the greyhound struggle, but we knew that a team effort was needed to succeed. So we decided to lay our case directly before the volunteers and seek their buy-in. A meeting was scheduled at the Jamaica Plain offices of the Massachusetts Society for the Prevention of Cruelty to Animals. If the MSPCA and animal advocates chose to abandon ship, then our story would likely end. We had no idea what to expect and were filled with equal measures of anticipation and dread.

Although the MSPCA did not seriously engage in the first greyhound ballot measure, by 2006, the shelter had become an essential ally. The organization had a strong team, led by CEO Carter Luke and Director of Advocacy Kara Holmquist. The MSPCA had been the leading voice on animal protection in the Bay State since 1868, and was an institution in the best sense of the word. Luke and Kara understood that they had a duty to resolve the greyhound racing question in Massachusetts, one way or another. Christine had a special relationship with Kara and credited her with being one of the inspirations, along with Boston Magistrate Judge Sarah Luick, for her decision to attend law school while still working full-time. Kara was also a long-distance runner, like Christine, so the two shared common interests outside of work as well.

At the meeting, Carey laid out the situation in stark terms. We did not yet have agreement from the Humane Society of the United States, which had always viewed our dog racing prohibition as risky. If the Humane Society remained unwilling to engage, we might have to collect the signatures and raise the necessary funds without its endorsement or backing. But the alternative was unthinkable: give up and let the greyhounds continue to suffer.

A sober discussion ensued, with advocates weighing all the pros and cons. Carey made it clear that we would have to be prepared to sacrifice for the greyhounds anew, after losing twice. Other volunteers offered similar concerns, but they also expressed a great willingness to try again. Finally, political strategist and longtime ally Avi Nelson of Reading made the motion to move forward. Avi had been a longtime Republican panelist on the groundbreaking debate program *Five on Five*, a well-known radio host on *WRKO*, and had served as one of the ten chief signers to officially file the second ballot question. His friendship and guidance were our secret weapons in the early days. After a long moment of silence, the voting began. One volunteer after another raised a hand in assent. Carter Luke himself voted yes, saying simply "It's just the right thing to do."

Volunteers Deb MacClaren, Kara Holmquist, and Pam Mazzuchelli sort signature pages at the basement office of GREY2K USA in Somerville, Massachusetts, 2008 (Christine A. Dorchak/GREY2K USA)

And just like that, we had chosen to launch a ballot question in Massachusetts for the third and final time. Carey insisted that Christine would need to give a new face to the campaign and become the spokesperson this time. As much as she loved to debate, she was not trained and would need a lot of practice in order to represent the greyhounds well. While Carey has always had a natural way with words, she would quite literally need to study and commit to memory every possible question and every answer, learn what to say and how to say it, all the while keeping a friendly demeanor. It was a tall order, but she rose to the occasion, spending hours in mock debates, many of these taking place on three-mile walks home with Carey. In the end, with a grueling schedule of countless interviews on radio and TV, community debates at town halls across the state, and newspaper reporters calling day and night, she grew to live and breathe her role.

Carey informed Wayne Pacelle and the Humane Society of the volunteers' decision to move forward, which forced the HSUS CEO to set aside plans for a different ballot question. By this point we knew what we had to do to succeed. Two failures had taught us well! We were ready for every legal pitfall, prepared for any grassroots conundrum, and intimately familiar with every false argument and dirty trick used by industry spokespeople. We did extensive message development, and preplanned the entire campaign. We identified strong and effective messages that accurately represented the animal welfare problems in dog racing. We built the largest grassroots network for greyhounds ever, and eventually amassed more than five thousand active volunteers and roughly a hundred local coordinators. We leaned heavily on the tools of old-school activism. We held weekly conference calls with our local coordinators to share ideas and resolve problems. "Yes on 3" was a well-oiled machine, and ready to win. We had now perfected several techniques that helped us to be more effective. For example, during signature gathering periods, we mailed a weekly postcard to every volunteer, which provided an update and underscored the need for continued petitioning. These postcards became increasingly urgent as the deadline neared, and the final missive was entitled RED ALERT. It was printed on rocket red cardstock, a truly disquieting hue that hurt the eyes of everyone who received it.

Meanwhile, big life changes were afoot. Christine lost Kelsey to cancer in June 2005. A large dog, Kelsey managed to live to the age of fifteen. To this day, Christine believes the faithful Black Russian Terrier stayed by her side as long as she could, supporting her all the way through law school. Kelsey's death left Christine in despair for years to come. Sometimes, she would just sit at her desk and cry in the middle of the day. Few people knew of her loss, because it was too hard for her to share the news.

An unhappy landlord let Christine know that she would no longer be allowed to have dogs, so that meant it was time to leave the one-room Boston apartment she had called home for twenty years. Despite her catastrophic accident, she loved her fourth-floor walk-up along the trolley tracks of Commonwealth Avenue. Carey, however, never quite saw the charm and was glad for the move. After Christine took the bar exam in February 2006, plans were made to move to Arlington, where the owner of our office building had rental units that welcomed dogs.

On November 11, 2007, Christine and Carey were married in a modest ceremony surrounded by friends, family, and board members, including Reverend Tom Grey as their officiant. Our greyhound Zoe, adopted in 2006 from the National Greyhound Adoption Program in Philadelphia, served as ring bearer. A year later, Christine completed another marathon and Carey earned the National Master title in chess, the culmination of many years of intense study. He had the unique honor of studying with world-famous chess instructor Jonathan Rowson, and was published in the preeminent American chess magazine, *Chess Life*. It was a wonderful and fulfilling period.

After we had collected and submitted the necessary signatures to reach the ballot for the third time, once more with an all-volunteer effort, George Carney again challenged our question before the Massachusetts Supreme Court. At the hearing, 79-year-old George told us we would have to "run for the roses" to beat him, a reference to the Kentucky Derby. He also told the *Taunton Gazette* that our measure had as much chance of becoming law that year as he did of playing for the Boston Celtics. Poor George, he had no idea how powerful the greyhound movement had become! Plus, Assistant Attorney General Peter Sacks was now the lead attorney defending our measure. Thanks to his thoughtful and even-handed advocacy, the Carney challenge was defeated. Sacks went on to become a judge himself after winning the fight to keep the greyhounds on the 2008 ballot.

Our volunteers were magical. The top signature gatherer, Jed Winer, collected a final thousand signatures in a single weekend, just before the deadline. He did it at tony supermarkets in Wellesley, a wealthy community west of Boston. In the end, Jed met his goal, but he became deeply depressed after dealing with all of the "Wellholes," as he referred to them. One man wouldn't sign the petition, saying he only cared about himself! Another volunteer, Anne Albanese, courageously spoke up about greyhound cruelty despite living only a few miles from Raynham Park. Her greyhound, Snake, became the official Greyhound Protection Act spokesdog. Mimi Ryerson from Chestnut Hill, a spunky lady in her 60s, would show up almost every day to take more petition pages and gather signatures for the dogs, rain or shine. Iris Feldman of Belmont served as one of our chief office workers and sorted petitions as they were dropped off by other volunteers. The multi-talented Jodie Wiederkehr, our campaign coordinator, kept everything humming. She was to go on and form her own organization, and eventually lead a campaign to ban carriage horses in Chicago.

Yes on 3 volunteers rally on the Boston Common, November 2, 2008 (Denise McFadden).

We now had extensive data about animal welfare problems at Massachusetts dog tracks. Thanks to the recordkeeping laws passed seven years earlier, we were able to show voters how racing greyhounds actually lived. More than eight hundred injuries had been reported to the state since 2002, nearly 80% involving dogs with broken legs. Other injuries included head trauma, seizures, paralysis, stroke, broken necks, and cardiac arrest. To counter us, the industry released video footage from inside the Massachusetts kennel compounds, showing a pro-industry adoption figure working as an assistant trainer. This was a misguided attempt to whitewash greyhound cruelty, but backfired when we used the same footage in the new Greyhound Protection Act television ads. Our new ads were the work of legendary producer and political guru, Deno Seder of Washington, DC.

When Deno and his son Jeorge came to Massachusetts for filming, a strange thing happened. After a full day of recording statements from GREY2K USA volunteers, they felt confident they had succeeded in capturing our grassroots spirit, but something was missing. That's when Jeorge noticed The Cage. At the time, we had a racetrack cage in the office. It had been sent to us by David Wolf, founder of the National Greyhound Adoption Program. At one point, a local reporter had expressed interest in writing a column while sitting inside it, hoping to give a greyhound's point of view, so to speak. The column never happened, and the cage was converted for use as a worktable in our tiny office. Finally realizing this was no ordinary table, Jeorge began to crawl inside it, shooting video. Something about it fascinated him. Weeks later, when we saw the first cut of the TV ad, it opened with the bars of that cage. Things were falling into place.

We raised six hundred thousand dollars, and almost every penny was spent buying TV time so that we could bring the lives and deaths of greyhounds right into voters' living rooms. We depicted the dogs' confinement and let them see injured greyhounds. We described and showed the actual diseased meat the dogs were fed, highlighting the nineteen hounds who died at Wonderland after contracting horse flu from it. We also called attention to the spate of canine cocaine positives at this same track in 2003 and 2004.

It looked like the long-awaited wave of change was coming. With state records in hand, thousands of active volunteers in the field, and a bit more experience under our belts, our hopes were high, or at least, cautiously optimistic. Some volunteers held bake sales, while others tabled and stood outside with signs at local events. They went door to door, leaving leaflets and speaking to their neighbors about the importance of ending dog racing. Telephone trees were activated, and email alerts went out each day. Then, on the weekend before the vote, there was a blessing of the animals at the Cathedral Church of Saint Paul on Tremont Street in Boston. Greyhound advocates brought their dogs and asked for divine intervention—as well as the votes of the parishioners. No opportunity to spread the word was missed in the last few weeks preceding election day.

Our proposal, again appearing on the ballot as Question 3, was brought home by a multitude of small acts of heroism. Importantly, more than a dozen lawmakers defied leadership and endorsed the measure. This was a real game changer in many ways, and something we would need to build on after the election.

Full-throated support came from near and far. Volunteer Paula Blanchard of Lexington wrote a passionate guest column for the *MetroWest Daily News* about her newly rescued greyhound, who was named Hope. Paula was an award-winning biographer and transcendentalist who lived a stone's throw from the battle that had started the American Revolution. She told readers how much the campaign meant to her and to Hope, a survivor of the Revere track. Her beautiful words spoke to the power of patriotism and the importance of sacrifice for a higher cause. Other key volunteers, all veterans of the animal protection movement, gave the greyhounds their all as well. Retired MIT scientist Margaret Law collected signatures in the snow, the rain, and the heat. Marion Penney and Rita Escor, both of the Brockton area, drove for two hours three times a week to answer phones and write thank-you notes. Julie Neubauer of Acton helped record the never-ending stream of track injury reports. Ann Greenwood served as the first official office assistant, followed by Anita Slayton of Revere and then Jess Weller, who also volunteered to hide the 2008 signatures in the basement of the nearby pottery shop where she worked. In 2000 and the years that followed, petitions and other documents were stolen from other campaign headquarters, which was a risk we could not take. Cathy Woodruff and her husband Morgan initially volunteered to secure signatures in their Cambridge storage facility, which started our practice of never leaving signatures in the office overnight.

There is one anonymous man who stands out in our memory. He was an older gentleman, seen standing in the middle of a busy intersection in Quincy Center on the day of the election. He was not an official volunteer or even known to us, but there he was, swaying precariously on the median while waving a handmade sign that read "Please vote for the dogs today." The campaign had truly taken on a life of its own.

Shortly before the election, we received unexpected encouragement from thousands of miles away. On August 23, 2008, the last of three dog tracks in Kansas held its final race and closed—permanently. Live racing had finally ceased after the tracks experienced a 95% decline in betting. Kansas is the home of the National Greyhound Association and the Greyhound Hall of Fame, so this was a major blow to the industry. That said, dog racing in the Sunflower State had experienced a very short shelf life. The first two tracks opened in 1989, almost sixty years after Florida first legalized dog racing and just as the activity had begun its downward spiral in other parts of the country.

Christine Dorchak and campaign volunteers celebrate the passage of Question 3 at
Jillian's in the Fenway, November 4, 2008 (Boston Globe)

November 4, 2008, felt like a dream. Thousands of people and
their dogs were stationed at the polls during the day. That night,
we had organized a vote watch party at Jillian's, the famous billiard
club across from Fenway Park. As we all showed up and nervously
shared the day's experience in the field with each other, there was no
shaking the deep fear in our hearts. Were the greyhounds going to
lose again, despite our best efforts? All we could do now was to wait.

Carey and Christine hovered over Denise McFadden's laptop
to watch the results. County by county, precinct by precinct, the
votes started coming in. Then, in a flash, it was over. At 8 p.m.,
with all polls closed, local TV stations began reporting that we had
won! Like magic, the Question 3 victory splashed across the giant
TV screens all around us. Some volunteers openly wept. Christine
and Libby Frattaroli hugged each other so hard that they fell to the
floor. The relief and the release from years of anxiety were palpable
among all the fifty volunteers who stood with us that night. The
next day, the *Boston Globe* featured a photo of a gleeful Christine

celebrating with her fellow activists. On the same cold night that Barack Obama made history by becoming the first Black president of the United States, the Massachusetts Greyhound Protection Act had won by 12%, carried twelve of fourteen counties, and received the approval of 290 cities and towns out of 351 statewide.

Of course, our story does not end here. The industry was so bitter in defeat that it did all it could to block us from helping with the transition of dogs from Wonderland and Raynham Parks. Local greyhound adoption groups were weaponized in a way never seen before. Kennel owners bullied them into silence and secrecy, promising easier access to dogs to those who would refuse to join our adoption coalition. Nevertheless, the number of 2009 adoptions broke all records and the cruelty and killing of greyhounds in Massachusetts was finally over.

Sadly, track workers were also convinced to work against their own interests. They rejected both the state job retraining program offered by Governor Deval Patrick and the funds and training available from the federal government's Rapid Response Team. Both had been announced right away, the day after the election. Christine also drafted a bill to create a new statutory fund to provide educational opportunities and financial assistance to track workers. The monies would be diverted from the subsidies once given to the track owners themselves. "An Act Providing Economic Opportunities for Greyhound Racetrack Employees," was filed by Representative Carl Sciortino of Somerville in January 2009, but the measure received absolutely no support from its intended beneficiaries. HB 1856 quietly died in committee.

Greyhound breeders also tried to sue their way out of the loss, when four of them decided to make a claim of election fraud. The Lynn District Court dismissed the matter out of hand. Then, in April 2010, the owners of the old Lynn Kennel Compound filed yet another suit, this time in Essex Superior Court. They claimed that since voters were not asked to outlaw horse racing, the ballot question was discriminatory and *not broad enough*. Ironically, this was the opposite of what George Carney had argued in 2006 when he succeeded by saying our ballot question was *too broad*—a juxtaposition that did not escape Christine. Kennel owners also demanded to be compensated for loss of property (i.e. their dogs). Associate Justice Timothy Q. Feeley rejected all these claims, finding that Question 3 effected no unconstitutional taking of property and was not violative of equal protection guarantees. The vote to end dog racing was fair and square and would stand.

On September 19, 2009, dogs raced around the iconic Wonderland oval for the final time. A few months later, on the day after Christmas, the last Massachusetts dog race was held at Raynham Park. Somehow, we had managed to defeat the titanic dog track barons of New England.

O'Mahoney cartoon celebrating the end of dog racing in Massachusetts, November 7, 2008 (Joe Mahoney/USA Today Network)

Chapter 8

A Vote for Amber

"Each of these dogs had a name, a mother, and siblings. They felt fear, and joy. Sadly, their stories, their names, and their fates have been lost to time."

—New Hampshire Senator Sheila Roberge

Unbeknownst to us, five weeks after the Massachusetts vote and on the far end of the earth, sweet little Brooklyn was born. As our Massachusetts miracle was blossoming into a political movement, his suffering was only beginning. While we fought for greyhounds in New England, Brooklyn was born in Australia, removed from his mother and siblings, and then shipped to China after failing as a racer. He was now living alone in a small, concrete cell with barred windows at the Canidrome. Help for him and his fellow hounds was still years away.

Back home, on the heels of our "Massachusetts Miracle" at the ballot box, we focused our attention on New Hampshire once more. Due to a shared media market, Granite State citizens had seen our Question 3 TV ads. This had a profound impact on the debate and when the legislature reconvened in January 2009, awareness was at an all-time high. We were determined to capitalize on this opportunity, and a bill to outlaw greyhound racing was refiled—this time by Representative Mary Cooney of Grafton. Cooney, who would eventually serve eight terms in the House, was clever, determined, and resilient. She was also very unassuming and had a quiet and kind demeanor. Her bill gained broad support in the legislature and won the endorsement of dozens of local animal shelters and animal protection organizations. Our first task was to reassemble the coalition we had built, which had been largely inactive for two years—although we had, in the interim, won passage of an important bill in 2008 to restore greyhounds to the state's anti-cruelty law. Cooney's bill was sent to the House Local and Regulated Revenues Committee, where we found a great deal of support. In a desperate but nonetheless successful move, dog track lobbyists convinced the committee chair to delay consideration of the bill for a year.

While the Cooney bill was pending, Steve Vaillancourt launched a separate assault. He approached his colleagues, who considered him an expert on fiscal matters, and asked them to end a state subsidy for greyhound drug testing as part of the state budget. When it became clear that this gambit was going to succeed, the dog tracks quickly abandoned their opposition and instead added language to the budget that ended the state mandate for live dog racing altogether! They could not afford to operate without the state handout, and their amendment ensured that they could remain open as hubs for simulcast gambling on horse and dog races taking place elsewhere, regardless of what happened with the Cooney bill to ban live greyhound racing. The decoupling and drug testing provisions were both quickly adopted.

Almost immediately after the budget passed, and the state mandate for dog racing repealed, greyhound racing ended in New Hampshire. There was no fanfare, only a few news stories romanticizing a cruel sport. The tracks could not turn in their licenses fast enough because, truth be told, they were losing money and the business they had worked so hard to protect was sinking fast. Overnight, the starting boxes went silent, and the kennel cages were emptied. A surprising thing we learned at this time was that when change happens, the sky does not open up with rainbows and light, no matter how great of a victory has been achieved! One day the struggle simply ends, and everyone moves on.

MPW10'06 AM 9:08 NHPMC

New Hampshire Pari-Mutuel Commission Greyhound Injury Report

Track: **SEABROOK Greyhound Park**   Date of Form: **APR 22 2006**

Greyhound's Registered Name: NO NGA PAPER "AMBER"

Tattoo Right: 84A   Left: 28546   Color: RED   Sex: F   Weight: 60 lb

Owner: DON JARRETT, P.O. BOX 985, SORRENTO, FL. 32776-0985
(352) 383-7951 (352) 516-3037
    Name   Business Address   Phone

Trainer: SHARON McCREERY 107 Seabrook NH 03874   N/A
    Name   Business Address   Phone

Kennel Operator: ADIOS KNL #7   Rt 107 Seabrook NH 03874   N/A
    Name   Business Address   Phone

Indicate where the injury took place on the track or;   3/8 Box 3/16 Box 7/16 Box

Other area: _____

5/16 Box

If the injury occurred while the greyhound was racing: UNOFFICIAL SCHOOLING

Track where injury occurred: **SEABROOK**   Date: **APR 21 2006** ☒ Mat ☐ Eve

Distance: 550 YDS   Grade: _____   Race: _____   Post Position: _____

Location of Injury on the Greyhound:

Specific type of Injury: FX. SKULL - MASSIVE BRAIN DAMAGE

Cause of Injury: RAN INTO THE RAIL - BEFORE RACE ENDED

Estimated recovery time: DECEASED

"I declare that, to the best of my knowledge and belief, the information provided on this form is true, correct and complete and acknowledge that knowingly making of a false statement on this form is punishable by law, including by the imposition of those penalties set forth at RSA 284:14-d, II"

Track Veterinarian: **Alan C. Zezula**   APR 22 2006
    Name (printed)   Signature   Date Signed

Witness representing NHPMC: _____   APR 22 2006
        Signature   Date Signed

Official Seabrook Greyhound Park death report of Amber, April 22, 2006
(State of New Hampshire)

But the New Hampshire campaign would not be completely over until commercial dog racing was outlawed and could never return. So in 2010, Representative Cooney's bill was considered again. It passed its House Committee in a near-unanimous vote of 15-2. This was the first time in the history of our organization that we had ever won the support of a legislative committee. HB 630 passed the full House on a voice vote, meaning it was considered non-controversial. But a final obstacle stood in the way, embodied in one man: Senator Lou D'Allesandro had fought for years to protect the racing industry, and he was absolutely determined to save it again. His was a personal crusade, and he fought with all of his strength, pleading with colleagues to reject our proposal. Senator Sheila Roberge fought back, calling in every favor she had to help the Cooney bill. On April 14, the day the measure reached the Senate floor, Roberge rose from her chair to give the most important speech of her career. In a soft but forceful voice, she told her colleagues about all of the greyhounds that had died in New Hampshire, including a dog named Amber.

> Four years ago, a one-year-old greyhound named Amber was taken out of her cage at Seabrook Greyhound Park. That morning, she was going to race for the very first time. It was a Spring morning in the middle of April, like the morning we woke up to today. Amber was owned by a Florida man that may never have even met her. She was raised on a breeding farm in yet another state, and at a young age, was hauled across the country so that she could race at Seabrook.
>
> At the track, she was kept in a concrete building along with hundreds of other dogs. These dogs lived in cages, and raced, so that people could gamble on them, like lottery numbers. Their cages were barely large enough for them to stand up or turn around.
>
> That morning, Amber's first race was also her last. Sadly, she ran into the racetrack rail, suffered massive brain damage, and died. Amber's story is tragic, but

it is not unique. Since 2005, nearly twelve hundred greyhounds have been injured while racing in our state, including dogs that suffered broken bones, paralysis, and cardiac arrest.

Over the past forty years, tens of thousands of greyhounds have raced in our state. Each of these dogs had a name, a mother, and siblings. They felt fear, and joy. Sadly, their stories, their names, and their fates have been lost to time. But we know they existed. Like Amber, many of these dogs suffered and died. They suffered broken legs and broken necks. Many were killed because they were one second too slow and could no longer make a profit. That is why I am voting 'yes' today, I am casting my vote for Amber.*

The chamber fell silent as Senator Roberge sat down. Then, in a voice vote, the New Hampshire Senate outlawed greyhound racing once and for all.

There were so many unexpected lessons that came from the New Hampshire struggle. We learned the value of taking an incremental approach, building on small but important victories to realize a larger goal. One of the most difficult tasks is finding a way to start and ensuring that each step helps reduce the cruelty of racing while also exposing it for what it does to dogs. Small advances, like injury reporting and striking subsidies, multiply and work together to create a new environment in which fundamental change becomes possible. Our victories in New England did not occur because of any ingenuity on our part. We worked very hard and tried to avoid mistakes, but in the end, we happened to be in the right place at the right time, ready to facilitate change for the greyhounds. As Tom Grey presciently said at the beginning of our journey, the industry always contained within itself the seeds of its own destruction.

---

* Roberge, Sheila. 2010. "NH State Senator Tells Lawmakers about Amber, a Greyhound Who Died in Her First Race." In-Person. Edited by GREY2KUSA. April 14. https://www.youtube.com/watch?v=iqw44LcUY7I.

Mike Trombley, Paul LaFlamme, and Mary Cooney still live in New Hampshire. After serving in the Senate for twenty-six years, Sheila Roberge retired and moved to Florida in 2012. She passed away in October of 2018, just nine days before voters in the Sunshine State joined her home state in outlawing dog racing.

In March of 2017, while Steve Vaillancourt was serving his tenth term in the House, he missed a House Finance Committee hearing. Police found him in his home, where we had died alone at the age of 65. In one of his last emails to colleagues on greyhound racing, he had written that, second only to passing a marriage equality bill, outlawing dog racing had been his proudest accomplishment because "No longer are dogs held hostage as the state subsidizes an industry that people have stated loudly and clearly that they oppose. Never have I had to deal with such an unethical industry. New Hampshire now joins Massachusetts whose voters by a tremendous margin decided to end dog racing. It only exists in a few pockets of states, mostly where animal cruelty is simply accepted as a way of life—think Michael Vick." It is no exaggeration to say that without the tenacity and determination of Steve, greyhound racing would not have ended in the Granite State.

Two months after Steve passed, Nancy Johnson died quietly in her home at the age of 67. She had been a smoker for many years, but had recently called Christine to let her know that she had quit and wanted to help us in Florida. Sadly, she made her contribution posthumously. In her last will and testament, she instructed that all proceeds from the sale of her home be split between **GREY2K** USA and the American Lung Association. Her generous foresight would give us the seed money to begin our biggest campaign ever the next year.

We were transformed by the fights to end greyhound racing in Massachusetts and New Hampshire. These battles gave us newfound faith in American democracy and forced us to be better advocates. Now we knew that change was possible if we worked hard enough and never gave up. Over the next decade, we applied what we learned to campaigns in other parts of the country, and eventually in other parts of the world. We also started to dream about ending greyhound racing in its biggest state: Florida. Home to two-thirds of all American tracks, it was truly the beating heart of the US dog racing industry.

CHAPTER 9

A RIBBON OF OPPORTUNITY

"Keep pressing grey2k . . . Do not allow them to play offense. Make them spend time and resources defending themselves instead of attacking the industry."

—Rory Goree

The closure of all the New England tracks provided real momentum. For the first time, we could advance our agenda in multiple states simultaneously. Christine would draft legislation and the lobbying push would begin. What had once been a single advocacy thread, or at most a handful of threads, now blossomed into a ribbon of opportunity.

We were developing our own method: a blending of grassroots activism, deep policy research, and modern political techniques all working together to reach a focused goal. Yet, simplicity was the key. What we had to do was show voters the way racing greyhounds live, using evidence from the industry itself, and ask them if *they* would treat their own dogs this way. We began to understand the industry better than it understood itself, and Carey provided *bona fide* information to both reporters and lawmakers alike.

This led to thousands of news stories about the problems associated with dog racing, and culminated in a comprehensive report called *High Stakes, Greyhound Racing in the United States,* which we released in 2015. Our white paper was based on thirteen years of public information requests and analysis, first performed by Christine and then transitioned over to multiple research directors over time. The days of Carey and Christine working in a one-room office, wearing ten hats each, were starting to end as GREY2K USA was able to bring in smart, young professionals to focus on key aspects of our daily work. Over the years, we had obtained tens of thousands of government documents related to injuries, drug positives, abuse cases, and other industry "dirty laundry." Director of Research Amelia Cook, who held an advanced degree in Animals and Public Policy from Tufts University, spent months assembling all of this data into a single document, the first ever of its kind. Meanwhile, Christine read everything she could about the history of dog racing, from friends and foes alike, and wrote the report's introduction. When we were finished, *High Stakes* was eighty pages long and contained nearly six hundred endnotes. We addressed every conceivable issue, from confinement and greyhound cocaine positives to racetrack injuries and deaths.

Regrettably, some of our best research was never given any public attention at all. In 2016, we completed an analysis of the number of greyhound puppies born according to the National Greyhound Association. We compared this to the number of dogs actually registered to race. To our horror, over a three-year period, 8,162 American greyhound puppies had simply disappeared into thin air. Multiple journalists interviewed Carey for a story, but none brought it to publication.

Over time, we gained credibility with reporters by providing data that was both accurate and well-sourced. If we did not know the answer to a question, we said so, and offered to come back with additional research. One of our board members, Caryn Wood of Arizona, submitted letters to the editor every time any news story on dog racing was published anywhere in the world. This helped educate mainstream audiences while also letting our opponents know that we were beginning to have a wide reach.

We also recognized how important it was to perpetually strengthen the organization after its near collapse in 2006. We came to realize that a successful political effort required constant care, evaluation, and reevaluation. To succeed, we had to build a strong vehicle to steer our work. Thankfully, we had the opportunity to consult with animal rights guru and philosopher Kim Stallwood. A native of England, he served as the Executive Editor of *Animals' Agenda Magazine from 1993 to 2002*, successfully campaigned against both vivisection and fur in his own country and worked closely with Ingrid Newkirk in the early days of PETA. The author of several insightful books about the movement, Kim was a true expert, and we were incredibly fortunate to have his friendship and guidance.

As time transpired and interest in our work grew, industry leaders felt increasingly threatened by the light we were shining on their decades-old practices. Greyhound breeders and their supporters began to create and spread a series of conspiracy theories. At various turns, we were supposedly pawns of anti-gambling groups, secret agents for casino interests, cynical con artists, and/or ideologues blinded by animal rights fanaticism. These attacks were propagated in self-created echo chambers under names like "Grey2K Lies." It mattered little that these false narratives were often internally contradictory. We have never known greyhound breeders to let logic get in the way of a good story! These dark forums also became a place where enmity festered. We were attacked in the most vicious and personal ways, and Christine's 1992 near-fatal accident became a particular obsession. Greyhound cruelty deniers obtained a copy of the police report of her accident, and posted photos of Christine in intensive care. They frequently joked about trains, usually accompanied by sexist slurs.

All this animosity rested on an ill-conceived strategy. For years, the NGA retained a political operative named Marsha Kelly, who claimed to have revived the image of the fur industry when it came under attack by animal advocates in the 1980s and 90s. Kelly urged her clients to attack ferociously and deny everything. In 2011, Rory Goree admitted this was intentional, telling dog track supporters to "keep pressing grey2k." "Force them into defense mode," he wrote. "Do not allow them to play offense. Make them spend time and resources defending themselves instead of attacking the industry." He also advocated for legislation to make racing documents private and suggested that any citizen organizations making public information requests should themselves become subject to Freedom of Information requests.

These forums of hate reassured racing insiders, easing the pain of watching the so-called glory days of dog racing fade away. Everyday people had turned against greyhound breeders. Many lawmakers abandoned them, and now even track owners were looking for the nearest exit. None of this was noticed or understood by our opponents, who kept doing and saying the same things and hoping for a different outcome.

While breeders circulated conspiracy theories, we continued to receive tips from industry informants about greyhound abuse. Sometimes they seemed to want to help, other times it was pretty clear that they were just bad mouthing the competition to settle their own scores. While we could not use these tips as more than hearsay, every phone call, email, text, and letter motivated us to keep working. In 2012, Carey was forwarded a firsthand account of the conditions at an Alabama racing kennel operated by Grant and Saul Cohen:

> I went down to Mobile to work for Hoosier kennel, WTF! Gina and me get there and we have 91 dogs, 9 doubles!! The nastiest shit I have ever seen. The dogs haven't been wormed in over 3 months, bitches in milk, one bitch has a broken leg up top doubled with another bitch! TOTALLY infested in ticks and fleas, pulled 62 ticks off one ear! Sores all over dogs, no antibiotics AT

ALL, NO vitamins, bitch pills, bleach, pine sole, NO MEAL!! The smell of piss and funk would knock you out the door. Hasn't been swept or cleaned in months!! I have never seen such deplorable conditions in my life!! EVER!! . . . I asked (Grant) for expense $ and he says can't send no $ till saturday (it's wednesday). I packed my shit and left.

Based on this confidential tip, and with supporting information from the NGA itself, Christine filed a 25-page complaint with the local district attorney. The DA declined to prosecute, stating that there was "no evidence of wrongdoing." Christine then wrote to Attorney General Luther Strange, but his office also refused to intercede due to "limited resources and other investigative priorities."

Jorge Hank Rhon, owner of the Agua Caliente dog track, June 13, 2006 (AP Photo/ David Maung, File, © 2006 AP)

Since its inception, the greyhound industry had bullied everyone it viewed as a threat, including adoption groups, lawmakers, and business competitors. But such coercive tactics did not work with us. We presented a unique threat because we could not be intimidated.

We had nothing to lose, which gave us a lot of courage! For example, in May of 2010, we learned that MIR Caliente was approved as a member of the American Greyhound Track Operators Association. The company was controlled by Jorge Hank Rhon, who owned Agua Caliente and had been the mayor of Tijuana. His was the only legal greyhound track in Mexico. At one industry conference, MIR Caliente was referred to as the "newest and most supportive member" of the AGTOA and was billed as the host of a lavish cocktail reception for attendees. We wrote to the Association, expressing our concerns and urging it to sever any relationship with Rhon.

Rhon had been repeatedly linked to the trafficking of endangered wildlife, and had been fined $25,000 in 1991 for his involvement in the illicit transfer of a White Siberian Tiger cub. He reportedly owned a liger and was detained by the federal government in 2011 after agents discovered 88 guns in his home. In our letter to the AGTOA, we cited published reports regarding the controversies that had shadowed Rhon for decades, including suspected links to drug cartels. A few weeks afterward, we received a response from Rhon's attorney. On behalf of "Mr. Hank," he demanded a full retraction and apology within ten days, threatening a multimillion-dollar lawsuit for non-compliance. For obvious reasons, we took this situation very seriously and consulted with an expert in the field. Christine obtained the assistance of renowned Boston attorney and free speech specialist Jonathan Albano, who found the language and tone of Rhon's claim appalling. He refuted every claim and made it painfully clear that Rhon would be paying his firm's very expensive legal fees if GREY2K USA were ever contacted again. Just as with Charlie Sarkis, we knew we could use anti-SLAPP protections to not only defend ourselves against Rhon but make him pay our legal fees. In effect, we bullied the bullies! We never heard from "Mr. Hank" or his lawyers again.

Because we were fighting a powerful industry with a long history of political influence, we had an obligation to know our legal rights and stand up for them. For example, we had a right under what is called the "Fair Use Doctrine" to use industry photographs and other materials, as long as we were not doing so for commercial purposes. What's more, permission was not required since we were engaged in a public debate about an issue of public concern, meaning that our work was protected by First Amendment freedom of expression guarantees. In other words, the fact that this involved political speech heightened our protections. But this didn't stop greyhound breeders from griping when their kennel photos and videos were introduced into the public debate and used as part of our educational and voter outreach. They liked to accuse us of "stealing" and filed multiple complaints with Google, YouTube, and Facebook under the Digital Millennium Copyright Act. Each time, Christine simply put on her lawyer hat and made them go away.

While we launched new campaigns, we also had to defend our hard-earned victory in Massachusetts. A few months after the 2008 election, we were called into the office of the House Ways and Means Chairman, Brian Dempsey. Dempsey had reached this powerful position by playing the game and doing the dirty work of one House Speaker after another. As soon as we arrived at his office, and with no introductions, Dempsey jumped right in and demanded that we agree to delay the implementation of our ballot question. He actually seemed to want to postpone it entirely by tying the effective date to ever-changing state economic metrics. Without missing a beat, we reminded him that the greyhounds had won by double digits and that we wouldn't accept any delay at all. The voters had spoken, and greyhound racing was going to end. Period.

Despite our bravado, we knew we had to act fast to protect Question 3. Our volunteers sprang into action and began to secure written commitments from Dempsey's Committee members to uphold the will of the voters. When we had promises in hand from a large majority, Carey informed Dempsey's Chief of Staff that he did not have the votes to delay or repeal our question. Outraged, the aide responded by saying that the "Chairman always has the votes if he wants them." These words served as a grim reminder of the cynicism and corruption that had sabotaged progress on Beacon Hill for so many years. In the end, we were forced into a compromise. In order to protect the live racing ban, we agreed to a further nine-month extension of remote wagering on dog races, referred to as simulcasting.

As expected, Chairman Dempsey's word was not to be trusted. He never honored our deal at all, pushing for a new extension on simulcasting with each legislative session. This modest setback reminded us that the political process is long and complicated, an endless sequence of victories, defeats, and unwanted compromise. For many years, we continued to fight for the full enforcement of Question 3, joined by faithful volunteers who testified at hearings, wrote letters, and made calls asking for the will of the voters to be honored in their state.

Nearly fourteen years later, and thanks to the persistence of Senate Majority Leader Cynthia Stone Creem, simulcast wagering on dogs was finally prohibited in the early hours of August 1, 2022. The addition of former state Representative Daniel Bosley to our team was a key reason for this long sought and happy outcome. He was so influential that Representative Michelle Dubois of Brockton herself co-sponsored our legislation, in complete defiance of her constituent and track owner George Carney. As the longtime Chairman of the Government Regulations Committee and a 24-year veteran of the House, Dan knew our issue well and regretted that he had never been able to overcome the influence of the dog track owners during his tenure. He made sure our language passed not once but twice by also adding it to a sports wagering bill. The final votes ending greyhound racing in Massachusetts were taken after midnight and in overtime, on the last day of a marathon session. Dan knew how to reach hearts and minds on Beacon Hill, providing the magic that the greyhounds needed to cross the last finish line.

Our victories in New England also led to another unexpected outcome. We were approached by more and more dog track owners, who for the first time expressed a willingness to close down active racetracks. We were suspicious of these direct overtures but felt an obligation to the dogs to see if a collaborative effort might produce results.

In neighboring Rhode Island, we were given an unexpected opportunity to collaborate with track ownership due to a bizarre sequence of events. Lincoln Greyhound Park had opened in 1977, and fifteen years later, was given the right to have slot machines—as long as dog racing continued and was subsidized by the owners. In 2003, the track was fighting for more slots while also trying to block a competing tribal casino. Two of its top executives were arrested for conspiring to bribe the Speaker of the Rhode Island House as part of their plot. The pair was later convicted and sentenced to three years in prison. In the wake of this scandal, the track owners were forced to transfer their interests, which were then sold to BLB Investors. Lincoln Greyhound Park was renamed Twin River and plans were made for a massive expansion. When these faltered in 2009, the track filed for bankruptcy. In court filings, Twin River admitted the losses it was taking on live racing, prompting Christine to reach out and begin working with track attorneys on drafting legislation. She also connected with animal advocate extraordinaire Dennis Tabella, the founder of a statewide group called Defenders of Animals. A military veteran and the well-known director of a network of community centers, Dennis was a quiet force for good at the capitol. Over the years, he had earned the respect of legislators from both sides of the aisle. Under his aegis, Rhode Island had passed one animal protection bill after another. When he agreed to join forces with GREY2K USA, it was a match made in heaven. At the time, there were many who did not appreciate our political methods, but Dennis was different. He understood the importance of working "in the process" and he got little GREY2K USA a seat at the table. The greyhounds were in good hands!

In the months that followed, we organized a joint rally at the State House, which was attended by volunteers from three states. They came with their rescued greyhounds and were determined to make Rhode Island the next state to ban dog racing. Later, when a hearing was called on our bill with little notice, GREY2K USA and Defenders of Animals were there to testify. Finally, on a hot summer night in 2010, the Rhode Island legislature voted to outlaw greyhound racing. Lawmakers applauded themselves for caring about dogs and for doing the right thing. Breathlessly, Christine and Dennis sat and watched from the upper gallery as dog racing ended in yet another state.

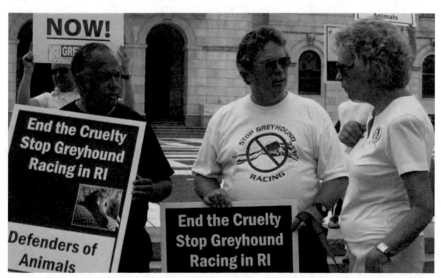

Dennis Tabella of Defenders of Animals, David French, State Representative Pat Serpa, and Jay Kirkus of Massachusetts (behind) at the Rhode Island State House, July 20, 2009 (Christine A. Dorchak/GREY2K USA)

At roughly the same time, Carey worked closely with track representatives in Council Bluffs, Iowa, who were eager to end the state racing mandate. The track already had casino gambling, and it was losing millions on greyhound racing. Bluffs Run was ready for a transition, which would help thousands of dogs while also being beneficial to the overall community. We were not the primary driver in the Iowa fight, but assisted whenever and however we could. Our job was to represent the interests of the dogs themselves, and we were upfront about this position with all sides of the greater gambling debate.

The Iowa fight was particularly challenging, due to the involvement of attorney Jerry Crawford. For many years, Jerry had served as counsel for the Iowa Greyhound Association. He was also a key figure in the Democratic National Committee, and a longtime "kingmaker" in Iowa politics. We had been on the verge of victory in the Hawkeye State for years, but every session, Jerry managed to stave off the seemingly inevitable outcome. In 2014, we finally passed a decoupling law, but it came with massive consolations for greyhound breeders. Under the plan lawmakers approved, greyhound racing ended immediately at Bluffs Run. The Iowa Greyhound Association, however, would have the right to itself operate the second track, located in Dubuque. The dogmen were promised an initial lease of only $1 per year and awarded a $72 million, multi-year "cessation fund" as well. Some of the monies would be awarded to trainers who left the industry immediately, with the rest being used for the operation of Dubuque. When the track reopened under IGA control, it immediately began losing money, but the rolling giveaway ensured it could survive for several more years. Of course, once the subsidies ended, the kennel operators announced that Iowa Greyhound Park was closing. During the track's last race on May 15, 2022, the winning greyhound suffered a heart attack at the finish line. His name was Superior Rex, and he was the last dog to die at this track.

By 2014, greyhound racing had also been outlawed in Colorado and Guam, and South Dakota allowed its authorization for live greyhound racing to expire. After the only dog track in Guam closed, Christine was among several advocates who helped rescue the surviving greyhounds. She was also given the honor of helping to draft the new law that would prohibit racing there once and for all. In Colorado, she and our board member James Flanagan worked with track lobbyists to pass a prohibition on commercial dog racing. James had recently stepped down as the President of Friends of Retired Greyhounds and could describe with authority the nearly 3,000 injured dogs that had suffered at racetracks in the area. Facing bankruptcy, the dog tracks had already closed, and the measure passed smoothly. As a result, the Centennial State became the 39th state to prohibit commercial dog racing in 2015. The bill was signed into law by then-Governor John Hickenlooper, who later became a US Senator. These successes, including the closure of VictoryLand in Alabama and the Jefferson County Kennel Club in Florida, hastened the economic collapse of the industry. Between 2008 and 2017, gambling on dog racing nationwide was cut in half, from nearly $1.1 billion to roughly $522 million.

In 2017, Wonderland was finally razed, construction workers reportedly unearthing greyhound skeletons around and behind the building. The track fixtures were auctioned off, and with the help of a local police officer and greyhound adopter, we managed to buy the very marquee that once greeted bettors at the main entrance. The chrome sign, a silver rectangle with the red and blue track logo, now hangs in our office for all to see.

The debate over greyhound racing was now a national struggle. As Carey toiled in Florida, Christine turned her focus to Arizona, to what many considered the worst dog track in the country. Tucson Greyhound Park was the veritable end of the line, a place where dogs that had failed elsewhere were sent to die.

CHAPTER 10

THE END OF THE LINE

"I am not going to let the press in because you are going to show it to thousands of people and we don't know how they are going to take it . . . I could show you the Taj Mahal and people would say that it is too religious."

—Tucson Greyhound Park Manager Tom Taylor

Where there had once been scores of greyhound racetracks in Arizona, going back to the Emprise days, now only Tucson remained. The conditions for the animals kept there were close to medieval, with dark and decrepit kennels and workers who repeatedly tested positive for illegal drugs. Revenue had fallen catastrophically, and racing only continued because of a complicated agreement, codified in state law, which required Tucson Greyhound Park to hold live races in order to operate a series of off-track betting parlors. This deal, called the Dome, had been worked out years earlier among all of the state's racetracks, and allowed the failing TGP to qualify for a "hardship tax credit" that could sometimes reach nearly $1 million a year.

Old Tucson Greyhound Park had always been mired in controversy. In 2008, a group of grassroots volunteers—led by former United States Attorney Susan Via—successfully collected signatures for a city-wide ballot initiative to outlaw the use of anabolic steroids in female greyhounds. After the question passed, track management flouted the new law, scheming to have a veterinarian take dogs a few feet across the South Tucson line for their routine steroid injections. When this subterfuge was revealed, advocates convinced Pima County to pass its own ordinance against the drugging of racing dogs. Not to be stopped, dog racers turned to the Arizona Racing Commission for help. The Commission told local authorities not to enforce the steroids ban, claiming that only the state had authority over this issue. Fortunately, this was a pyrrhic victory that only inflicted great damage on Tucson Greyhound Park's public image.

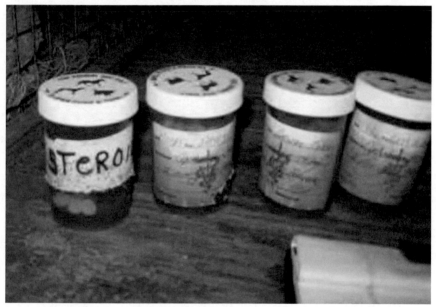

Bottles of steroids at the Tucson Greyhound Park kennels, February 26, 2016
(Pima County Inspection Report)

What followed was a steady drumbeat of scandals that attracted the ire of elected officials such as Tucson City Council Member Steve Kozachik. In 2010, an Arizona greyhound breeder had his license revoked after an inspection of his property found a dead greyhound and multiple starving dogs, some so thin they weighed less than twenty pounds. One was so physically weak that he could not move at all. We followed this revelation with our own undercover video exposé of life inside the kennels, which aired statewide. This was to trigger an official government report in June 2011 that confirmed the filthy and inhumane conditions for racing dogs at TGP. Images of filthy, feces-laden floors and blood-covered refrigerators made big and bad headlines for the track. In yet another episode in October, a greyhound trainer was fined $1,000 for failing to care for his dogs. Days later, a separate trainer was fined after the dogs he brought to race were found to be covered from head to tail with fleas. In March of 2012, a state inspection report also documented scores of ticks crawling up the walls of the onsite racetrack kennels. Three months later, the track was forced to cancel races after three trainers tested positive for drugs and one kennel operator refused to be tested at all. TGP was buckling under the weight of its own misdeeds.

As scandals continued to emerge, General Manager Tom Taylor took it upon himself to go before the media with one hair-brained excuse after another. He was ill-equipped to defend against the terrible conditions at the track. For instance, following the release of our undercover investigation showing muzzled dogs being warehoused in small, dirty cages, Taylor told a local television station that the track was an "ideal place for dogs." He went on to claim that our investigators had seen "what they wanted to see," but when asked, refused to open the kennels to reporters. Taylor's defense of the indefensible was bizarre. He compared the track to a work of art, on par with the "Mona Lisa and Taj Mahal." But when asked if he would keep his own dog at TGP, he said "of course not!"

Tucson Greyhound Park became a national flashpoint when Skechers contracted to film its 2012 Super Bowl ad at the venue. The company was going to put a happy face on dog racing, and we just could not allow that. One of our intrepid volunteers provided photos of a visiting production team installing new landscaping and colorful signage to cover up the terrible condition of the real track, which we used to write to the company with a request that it admit its mistake and cancel the ad. We began sending out Tweets featuring a dog named Hope who had competed at TGP more than 130 times. This little fawn dog had survived racing in temperatures topping 100 degrees, long confinement in a small cage, and regular injections of steroids to keep her "in the running." Receiving no response from spokesperson and investor Mark Cuban, we organized weekend-long demonstrations outside Skechers stores nationwide. This led to a crush of media attention, forcing the company to shelve its expensive campaign after just one broadcast. In the years since, the footwear monolith has gone out of its way to support animal welfare issues, which we like to think of as a bit of penance for the greyhounds.

Meanwhile, Christine began leading our legislative fight to dismantle Arizona's pari-mutuel laws which required that live races take place throughout the year. In 2010, her first decoupling bill failed to pass the Arizona legislature because track owners refused to support it. Two years later, we supported TGP's own version of the legislation, which called for live racing to be reduced to one hundred calendar days, with an opportunity for full decoupling once the dogmen agreed to the change. This was a step in the right direction, but ultimately unworkable given the determination of the kennels to remain open.

In 2013, we won a key victory when lawmakers passed a measure, signed by Republican Governor Jan Brewer, requiring the reporting of greyhound injuries and deaths. This information had always been a closely held secret by kennel operators, but we could now begin publicizing the full extent of the problem. The new records described 139 injuries in the first full year, including 45 dogs that suffered broken bones and two dogs that died while racing. One dog was even electrocuted when he fell onto the rail one Friday night in March of 2014. Greyhounds suffered broken backs, head trauma, heat stroke, puncture wounds, paralysis and seizures, and scores of broken legs. The fastest dogs on earth were then "euthanized" because they could no longer earn their keep. Christine's visit to the track one Friday night proved that this cruel exercise was occurring with no one watching. She found the bleachers empty—the only spectators being two ex-teachers who had come to see the "beautiful dogs." Assorted drunks watching horse races at the bar completed the pitiful scene.

The same year, greyhounds caught the interest of investigative reporter Matthew Schwartz. Widely known for his interview with serial killer David Berkowitz, aka "the Son of Sam," Schwartz had recently moved to Arizona from New York City and was doing special segments for *News4Tucson*. He publicized the track's losses and the sketchy tax credits that were keeping it afloat. After attempting to obtain comment from track manager Dale Popp, he found himself physically tossed from the property—something he was glad to broadcast to his audience that night. He also hounded two kennel operators, William "Willie" Eyler and Randell Graham, who had been involved in a scheme to drug dogs and refused to take drug tests themselves. When approached by Schwartz for their side of the story, Eyler gave him the finger and drove off, nearly hitting the reporter in his hasty retreat. Eyler later had his racing license revoked after one of his dogs tested positive for an anabolic steroid. Track official Jennifer Harger was also suspended, after testing positive for cocaine. Schwartz's reporting truly underscored the seedy and criminal nature of what was happening at the track.

In 2015, we had the good fortune of enlisting the aid of a dapper lobbyist named Michael Preston Green. This Cary Grant-like figure, in his impeccable suits and gleaming silver hair, was widely celebrated as the dean of Arizona's lobbying corp. Green was a lawyer who had worked in the capitol for nearly fifty years, successfully addressing a wide range of issues such as tort reform, healthcare, alcohol regulation, housing, energy, transportation, and mining. He was deeply respected and well liked. Presented with Christine's massive briefing book on the issue, which traced the initial authorization of racing in the state and detailed the present-day Dome agreement, he felt that he could help negotiate a compromise among the stakeholders. The fact that TGP was losing more than $500,000 a year on live racing convinced Green that we had a viable path. He teamed up with Representative John Kavanagh, an outspoken Republican from Fountain Hills, to champion the bill. We learned later that Green had been intending to retire that year, but decided to stay on for a good cause

Michael Preston Green celebrates the last day of racing in Arizona, June 25, 2016
(Timon Harper)

When racing supporters learned of our negotiations with track owners, the greyhound industry asked Rory Goree to gum up the works. Undeterred, we sent a letter to all seven adoption groups in the state, including his, offering financial support and asking for their help in accepting dogs when the track closed. By this time,

Rory was a member of the Arizona Racing Commission, so he was in a great position to protect the *status quo*. He openly lobbied against the bill, a rare act by a state official. He and his industry friends also created a handout describing our "fictions" about dog racing. But it didn't matter. A bill to completely outlaw greyhound racing passed in the House 54-0 and in the Senate 28-0 on May 8, 2016. Goree could not secure even a single vote in opposition! Governor Doug Ducey signed the measure into law five days later, stating that "Greyhound racing has run its course in Arizona. It's heartening that these beautiful dogs will soon be off the track and in loving homes."

Missula, Flash, Gidget, Robyn and Ed from Tucson Greyhound Park arrive in California, July 15, 2016 (Homestretch Greyhound Rescue)

The wonderful advocates who had worked for years to close Tucson Greyhound Park were elated when they heard the news, and the parties that followed lasted for several weeks. The ultimate reward, though, was when Christine and Caryn Wood were given the opportunity to oversee the exodus of hundreds of Arizona hounds into loving homes. The handwritten thank you letter from Representative Kavanagh celebrating the victory reminded Christine once more that the greyhounds would always have thoughtful friends on both sides of the aisle.

But while activists celebrated a hard-won victory, gentle Brooklyn still sat alone in his cage at the Canidrome, day after day, waiting for a helping hand.

CHAPTER 11

RESCUE BROOKLYN

"The most important thing now, besides the adoption of
Brooklyn, is to stop the killing."

—Albano Martins of ANIMA Macau

Macau is a land of contrasts, a small coastal nation in the South
China Sea that, for centuries, was claimed by both Portuguese and
Chinese sovereigns, but has now become a semi-autonomous state.
On one side of the Lotus Bridge, there exists a wealthy gambling
mecca and on the other, a shanty town where the casino workers
and other laborers live. It is one of the most densely populated areas
in the world, yet the southern end of this tiny nation is a tropical
paradise with areas that are still quite wild and lush. For decades,
Macau was home to the only legal dog track in China, the Yat Yuen
Canidrome; it had initially opened in 1931, then closed seven years
later due to a lack of interest, only to then reopen in 1963. According
to a 2011 news story in the *South China Morning Post*, high numbers
of unwanted Australian greyhounds were exported to the facility
by unscrupulous breeders trying to squeeze a few more dollars out
of them. The track had no adoption program, and every dog that
was sent there died. The Canidrome was a "no exit" destination
for some 400 greyhounds a year. The process was as coordinated
as it was calculated and cruel: thirty dogs would be shipped in each
month, and thirty dogs would be killed to make room for them.
When Christine saw the news report about this tragic situation, she
could hardly believe what she was reading. She put the article down

in shock and blurted out, "We have to shut this terrible place down. This is the worst dog track in the world!" Carey wondered aloud, how would we ever manage to close down a Chinese-controlled racetrack from a small basement office in Somerville, Massachusetts? But there was no changing Christine's mind.

In October of 2011, GREY2K USA Board Member Charmaine Settle agreed to visit Macau and inspect the track. She found a broken-down facility with old plastic red seats and a small, dirty "VIP" section. As she arrived in the afternoon, Charmaine also saw groups of dogs being walked around the property. She was witnessing one of the two short periods that the six hundred Canidrome greyhounds were let out of their cages per day, though she did not know it at the time. She felt crushing grief while watching this sad parade, knowing that many of the dogs she saw that day would soon be dead. Charmaine took photographs of the greyhounds, including one of a white dog with brown patches who had huge, soft eyes peeking through his wire muzzle. The letters "LYN" could be seen on his collar. Who was this striking dog, and what was his story?

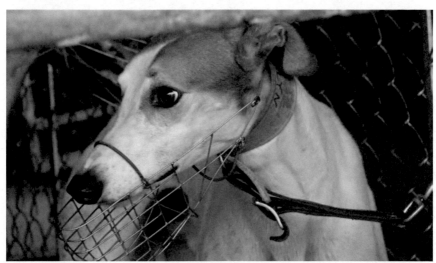

Brooklyn muzzled at the Canidrome in Macau, October 19, 2011
(Charmaine Settle/GREY2K USA Worldwide)

While in Macau, Charmaine also sought out a meeting with Albano Martins. An esteemed economist educated in Lisbon, Albano was charismatic, compassionate, and highly strategic. He had built strong relationships with local luminaries, including the former President of Macau as well as casino magnate Steve Wynn. Albano leveraged these connections to help animals in need and ran the only true shelter on the peninsula, saving hundreds of companion animals a year. But strangely, he did not know much about the Canidrome. After hearing Charmaine's account, he enthusiastically offered to help. Over the next few years, he would join our Board of Directors and lead an intense lobbying effort against the track, all in the face of continuous death threats.

After Charmaine returned home, she provided a detailed report alongside the photographs she had taken. In the GREY2K USA office, we looked at these images for hours, including the mysterious "LYN" greyhound. Looking at the gentle face, we realized it might be possible to build a movement around this single, striking photo. We worked to identify the dog, and found the only greyhound that was a possible match: a two-year-old boy named "Brooklyn." In mid-November, we sent a letter to the Canidrome, asking for the opportunity to adopt him. Letting one dog live, we argued, would be a great first step in a cooperative effort to help all of the dogs. Weeks passed, and we received no response. Brooklyn seemed to disappear from track records during this time and we presumed he was likely dead, one of the unlucky thirty that month.

Determined to give this beautiful dog a voice, we launched what became known as the "Rescue Brooklyn" campaign. Our Communications Director Danielle Festa designed mock "Missing" posters, culminating in a ten-country candlelight vigil to #CloseTheCanidrome. Across the world, people held up Brooklyn's image and called on the track to set the greyhounds free. This collective plea was widely publicized, and even reached reclusive spiritual leader Supreme Master Ching Hai, who offered the track $10,000 for Brooklyn's safe release. Like ours, her overtures were ignored. Meanwhile, Albano Martins began a delicate years-long diplomatic effort to convince the Macau government to shut down the Canidrome. This proved to be difficult as Stanley Ho, who owned the facility, was immeasurably powerful. His wife, Angela Leong, was a sitting lawmaker in the Legislative Assembly of Macau. Albano was smart and patient, however, and extremely methodical. He enlisted the help of former heads of the government, and never gave up.

Volunteer Chelsea Conlin of Nevada hangs "Missing" poster for Brooklyn, October 2013 (Chelsea Conlin)

Over time, the Macau fight became the centerpiece of a growing international strategy to help greyhounds. In 2009, Christine had flown to Washington DC to meet with a government delegation from South Africa. She provided extensive documentation as to the humane and economic problems associated with dog racing across the globe, helping to prompt the panel's decision not to legalize dog racing. Meanwhile, Charmaine inspected racetracks in several countries and documented their operations. In Argentina, she witnessed straight-course dog races that were held in an open field, and in Vietnam, she toured the Lam Son dog track and its huge breeding compound.

In September of 2012, Carey and Christine made their first international trip and met with UK greyhound advocates Trudy Baker of Greyt Exploitations, Lucinda Read of Greyhound Compassion, and Joe Duckworth of the League Against Cruel Sports. A decade earlier, the League had won passage of the Hunting Act which banned the hound hunting of animals (including foxes, deer, and mink) and had also ended greyhound coursing, the predecessor of modern commercial dog racing. The moment we sat down with Joe and his team, we sensed a kinship. The League was politically engaged, organized, sophisticated, and very effective. This was the type of organization we hoped to become. In that first meeting, Carey took a gamble and asked if Joe would consider authoring a joint report on greyhound racing in the United Kingdom. To our surprise and delight, he agreed on the spot. At the time, no major UK animal welfare group was openly opposed to dog racing—but the League was ready to take a stronger position.

While in the UK, we also met Clarissa Baldwin, who headed the Dogs Trust, a large national dog adoption charity. Clarissa had taken a particular interest in greyhound welfare and formed the Greyhound Forum, a working group that brought together animal welfare groups and industry representatives, including the Greyhound Board of Great Britain. Clarissa seemed to view the Forum as a way to push animal welfare reforms from within the industry. Racing officials, meanwhile, used the Forum to co-opt the animal protection community and prevent the idea of a prohibition from ever gaining ground. Grassroots groups were distrustful of the Forum, and of Clarissa in particular. From their perspective, the groups with money and influence were doing very little to fight for the dogs. There was also another obstacle that divided rank-and-file activists from the large groups. Some grassroots greyhound groups had a murky relationship with actual animal liberation groups and their intellectual leader, Ronnie Lee. Ronnie had a passion for ending dog racing, which discouraged established groups from working on the issue. While these philosophical differences festered, greyhounds continued to suffer and die. Within this context, we sought to build bridges with both the grassroots community and the established groups. It was at this time that we found a key ally in the RSPCA's International Director, Paul Littlefair, who was doing groundbreaking animal welfare work in China and had earned the trust of Beijing.

Upon returning home from the UK, we did a lot of soul-searching about the future of the organization. Just as we had felt a calling to transform our original state ballot initiative committee into a full-throttled national effort, we believed it was time to grow again. The cruelty of greyhound racing had no borders, and while it was an American invention, it had become a global problem. That said, we realized that if we were to accept an international mission, we would have to do so in the spirit of cooperation. We hoped to join hands with other advocates across the world.

So in 2013, we relaunched as GREY2K USA Worldwide. The announcement was made on October 12 while in the presence of close supporters and allies, including Joe Duckworth. He had personally flown over from London to begin work on our joint UK report and to meet with our supporters. A year later, in October of 2014, we flew over and joined the League in releasing, *The State of Greyhound Racing in Great Britain, a Mandate for Change.* Debuted at a formal event in the Winston Churchill room at Westminster, it documented multiple animal welfare problems including greyhound injuries, deaths, drug positives, and kennel conditions. The report called for a series of specific reforms and closed with the assessment that "greyhound racing has no place in a nation that values animal welfare as highly as Britons do." Just like that, the League had formally taken a position against commercial dog racing. This was one of those moments when we truly felt like we were living through history, and that we had a small role in a larger struggle for the greyhounds.

Four months after our return from London, the course of the greyhound debate changed forever. On February 15, 2015, Australia's premier news program, *Four Corners*, released footage of barbaric live lure training, in which greyhounds chased, tortured, and killed small animals including piglets, possums, and rabbits. Scores of greyhound trainers were shown in the footage, which had been secretly captured at breeding farms in Victoria, Queensland, and New South Wales. Overnight, the Australian racing industry was thrown into complete disarray. Multiple industry officials were fired or resigned. State governments across Australia launched investigations, including a New South Wales panel headed by the former High Court of Australia Justice, Michael McHugh. Amid this turmoil, we made our third major international trip, traveling to Australia, New Zealand, Hong Kong, and Macau. As with our original visit to the United Kingdom, this was an opportunity to meet advocates and learn about conditions on the ground.

In New Zealand, we stayed with researcher extraordinaire Lynn Charlton and inspected the Manukau dog track in Auckland. Races were running, but the place was practically empty—which meant we stuck out like a sore thumb. Not surprisingly, the manager asked us to leave, but not before we had already taken photos and exchanged a few choice words with a father who had brought his young son to the track.

In Australia, we spent a day with Hayley Cotton and Mark Meaden, the daring activists who had filmed the live lure training that aired on *Four Corners*. Without any assistance from professional organizations or media, Hayley and Mark spent months clandestinely documenting horrific animal cruelty, including incidents in which baby animals watched their mothers ripped apart by greyhounds during training. We felt a great sense of awe in their presence, and the grief of witnessing such terrible cruelty firsthand. We met with many other advocates and organizations while Down Under, including Glenys Oogies and Lyn White of Animals Australia, the Green Party, the Animal Justice Party, Animal Liberation New South Wales, Friends of the Hound, Greyhound Liberation Queensland, Sentient, and the Greyhound Equality Society. We were also granted a meeting with Scott Parker, Chief Executive of Greyhounds Australasia. Scott was relatively new and hailed from the world of basketball. He had genuinely been appalled at the barbarism exposed by *Four Corners*. Scott gave us a preview of the reforms he intended to introduce, including vast reductions in greyhound breeding. Christine shared with him some of the injury reporting legislation we had passed in other places, and we all found the conversation to be very positive. We publicly applauded Scott's intentions for positive change, but we were not surprised when greyhound breeders and trainers rejected his ideas and chastised him for even speaking with us.

While in New South Wales, we had the honor of meeting Green Party MP John Kaye and Senator Lee Rhiannon, both of whom made a profound impression on us. They ushered us into an ornate chamber right in the heart of Parliament. We sat and strategized about ending dog racing while sitting in velvet armchairs around a magnificent ebony table. Heavy gold curtains gave the room a kind of grandeur that was only matched by the precious paintings and bronze statues all around us. Was this really happening, we wondered?

Before the live baiting scandal, John and Lee had been some of the only lawmakers to give greyhounds a voice. John's mother had dedicated her life to ending commercial whaling and he recalled to us the planning meetings that had occurred in his house when he was a child. John was enthralled about our fight in the United States and spoke with us for hours about the positive force we would bring together in his country. He introduced us to Mark Pearson of the Animal Justice Party, who would play a key role in future campaigns.

After departing from Australia, we rested for a couple of days in Hong Kong, before traveling to Macau for an international roundtable hosted by ANIMA. Albano Martins had secured the participation of delegates from throughout Asia, including the Capital Animal Welfare Society, which was leading the fight against the dog meat trade in China. We talked through the next steps and Albano updated us on his personal lobbying to convince the government to close down the Canidrome. Procedurally, the path was simple: the track sat on a vast expanse of land that was owned by the government and leased to the Ho Family. Fortunately, this lease was about to expire. Despite this advantage, winning the Canidrome fight was not easy. The track owners were both powerful and dangerous, and if Albano could convince the Chief Executive to shutter the facility, it would have to be done in a way that allowed the family to save face. Albano used our conference to show the government how much international support he had, and we were granted a meeting with the Mayor of Macau. This formal event was held in a palace that had been built in 1849 by Portuguese interests and now served as Macau's Government Headquarters. Beautiful murals adjourned a grand staircase that led us to a glorious upper salon rich with ceramics and priceless paintings. We were invited to sit along one side of a long ceremonial table, where writing pads and sharpened pencils were waiting. The officials arrived and seated themselves across from us. Hot tea was served to all. Once again, we felt as though we were living in a dream.

The conversation that afternoon followed a careful protocol: each side gave an opening statement, which was repeated by

Albano Martins, August 9, 2018 (Anthony Wallace/AFP via Getty Images)

translators in Mandarin and in Portuguese, and then each person was allowed to make a short statement. Closing statements from each side followed. Albano spoke first, then Christine, then Paul Littlefair, who had joined our coalition on behalf of the RSPCA. Afterwards, we retreated to an open area of the large chamber so that official photographs could be taken. Christine and Albano were called aside and given a private audience with the Mayor, who told them (in Portuguese) that he "was on their side." He said that our arguments had been accepted by the Chief Executive, and that the Canidrome would be ordered to close in due time, once the track owners were given an opportunity to bow out gracefully. What a great moment this was, and what a great lesson in international relations for Christine!

We spent the next day visiting Albano's three-story shelter, meeting the hundreds of dogs, cats, and rabbits he had saved. After a final breakfast meeting with Albano and Paul in one of the few non-casino hotels on the peninsula, we returned home, grateful for the many new friends we had made and feeling optimistic about our growing campaigns. But just as we settled back into the office again, we discovered that our computer network had been hacked. A cybercriminal had accessed Carey's computer remotely and stolen massive amounts of data. The attack was initially traced back to a server in Ukraine, although it seemed to have actually originated in China. After the thief downloaded thousands of important files, including strategy documents, a plethora of harmful viruses were uploaded into our system—including a ransomware program that demanded $800 for their removal. Experts told us the attack bore a strong resemblance to those made by the Russian government in the lead up to the 2016 American Presidential election. To this day, we don't know the identity of the culprit and perhaps this doesn't matter. But this was our first politically motivated assault, and we knew the stakes were now much higher for all of us.

Over the next few months, the Australian debate raged on. Industry investigators were the targets of gunfire, including a drive-by shooting at the home of Racing Victoria's Chief Steward. The McHugh inquiry heard testimony that as many as 17,000 greyhounds were killed each year in New South Wales alone, and that 90% of trainers were using live baiting. Dr. Liz Arnott, who would later travel to our office, told the panel that stewards had been instructed against disclosing greyhound injuries and deaths in an attempt to block her fact-finding. The Australian media also began to report on the export of Australian greyhounds to the Canidrome. Scott Parker and Greyhounds Australasia responded by creating a greyhound passport system that disallowed transport to the peninsula. While this semi-state body did not have the power to enforce its new restriction, and the country's Prime Minister denied repeated requests to act, the stage was set for a blockade by Australian airlines that would come in December of 2015. The sickening cycle of unwanted greyhounds sent to their deaths in Macau was about to end and soon, Stanley Ho would run out of victims.

In January of 2016, tragedy struck when John Kaye was diagnosed with cancer. We were devastated, as was everyone who knew and loved him. After a valiant five-month fight—during which he was still calling out the government from his hospital bed—John passed away on May 6, 2016. Weeks later, in a meeting with the Animal Justice Party, New South Wales Premier Mike Baird admitted that he regretted not listening to John about the severe problems in greyhound racing and vowed to take up the cause.

On June 16, 2016, Michael McHugh delivered his report to the government, which found "overwhelming evidence of systemic animal cruelty, including mass greyhound killings and live baiting." Four days later, a delegation from Greyhounds Australasia visited our office to discuss the state of dog racing in the United States. We were completely candid and had a long talk about the inherent problems associated with racing, including confinement and injuries. In early July, Premier Baird held a press conference to announce the news that his government intended to outlaw commercial greyhound racing. The industry rallied its forces, but their efforts were for naught. The government rammed through a prohibition, which won final passage in August. This was a stunning advance, but we knew that it needed to be protected. We warned our allies to be vigilant, to engage in electioneering and insulate the new law by helping the campaigns of humane-minded legislators. Unfortunately, they simply assumed the battle was over.

Meanwhile, on June 30, 2016, the Macau government officially announced that the Canidrome's lease would not be renewed and that the owners had two years to relocate or close down. Everyone knew that there were no real relocation options on the tiny peninsula, but this "choice" allowed the Ho family to save face. All of Albano's careful work, as supported by advocates around the globe, had succeeded! We immediately began organizing what would be called the "Macau Airlift" of 532 surviving dogs to freedom. This involved a massive fundraising and organizational structure, with more than 100 groups from around the world signing up to receive dogs.

Back in Australia, the greyhound industry engineered a massive backlash that was led by militant right-wing talk show hosts Ray Hadley and Alan Jones. These pundits hammered the government every day, decrying the dog racing ban and trying to shred McHugh's credibility while also attacking the evidence of greyhound cruelty. Most of their arguments were nonsense, but it made great radio and was highly effective in stirring up unrest. In October, Rupert Murdoch's News Corp began purchasing businesses related to greyhound racing, including Punters.com.au, while his *Daily Telegraph* led the chorus of voices calling for the ban to be reversed.

This was a very busy time for the organization. Beginning in early 2016, Christine took three more trips to Great Britain and Ireland in an effort to support the work of greyhound advocates and lawmakers in these key countries. Then in October of 2016, we held the first-ever Greyhounds Around the Globe conference in Florida, attracting participants from not only around the country but around the world. Representatives from Australia, Belgium, Hong Kong, Italy, Macau, Spain, and the UK participated. For the first time, international greyhound advocates were literally sitting down with Americans to strategize for the dogs.

As 2016 drew to a close, Australian greyhound racers found an opportunity to embarrass the government after Nationals Member of Parliament Andrew Gee resigned, leaving an open legislative seat. The Nationals had formed a conservative coalition government with Premier Mike Baird and the Liberal Party, and it was this coalition that had backed the racing prohibition. Pro racers seized the moment and worked to replace Gee with Philip Donato, a member of an extreme, minor party known as "the Shooters, Fishers, and Farmers." When their gambit succeeded, this one election took Baird out of power and by April 2017, the ban was overturned. Not only had the greyhound racing industry come back from the dead, it had done so by bringing down a sitting government! This setback was absolutely heartbreaking, and we knew it was an inflection point for the entire animal welfare movement in Australia. Thankfully, the greyhounds did win some consolation when the Australian Capital Territory voted to outlaw commercial dog racing the following November. This victory was led by the Australian Royal Society for the Prevention of Cruelty to Animals and its dogged CEO, Heather Neil. She had been one the presenters at our Florida conference, and we treasure her friendship to this day.

In July of 2018, the Canidrome officially closed. The happy news traveled the world, and Albano was given access to the dogs for the first time. To his horror, he found hundreds of dogs living in isolation, wasting away in dark cells. Most greyhounds had no bedding at all and slept on hard concrete. The dogs had serious health issues, but he resolved to help as many as he could. A large team of volunteers had come with him to assess the dogs, give them their first blankets and hugs, and provide veterinary care. As Albano walked through the depressing compound, he spotted a thin, white and brown dog peering through the rusty bars of a darkened cell. At first, he could not believe his eyes. He had found Brooklyn. The face of the #ClosetheCanidrome campaign was still alive! He immediately emailed Christine, who burst into tears at the news. His one-sentence message read: "Guess who I just petted?"

One of the volunteers who arrived to help the surviving dogs at the Canidrome was Robin Reich, who lived in the state of Washington. She was a trained photographer and longtime greyhound advocate. She spent time with the terrorized dogs, walked them, and took as many photos as she could. The dogs were so bored that they scratched the walls and chewed on the bars of their cages until their mouths were full of blood. They even bit themselves out of stress. Robin saw old dogs who had somehow survived this hell for years alongside young dogs who had literally been born in their cells. The first time Robin saw Brooklyn, he was playing with his food. His kibble was all over the dirty floor, and she marveled at how he could be so fussy after nearly ten years of deprivation. Years later, she described him as gentle, calm, easy going, and funny. Brooklyn was a favorite among volunteers, and every day Robin worried that he wouldn't live long enough to be rescued. Several dogs didn't make it, including a dog named Midnight Terror. Robin held him in her arms as he died, his body shaking uncontrollably while suffering from septic shock. Midnight Terror was one of fifteen dogs who died before they could be given a second chance.

Months passed, and preparations were made for Brooklyn to take his second overseas trip, this time to the United States. This long-suffering hound would finally get the second chance he deserved after spending nearly a decade imprisoned at the Chinese death track.

So many people were now giving the greyhounds a voice, all part of a powerful movement that had spread across the world while Brooklyn sat alone in his cell. People were holding marches in Dublin, submitting letters to the editor in New Zealand, and protesting at tracks in Great Britain. And the most fantastical, consequential fight of all was taking place in Florida. In fact, the campaign to end greyhound racing in the Sunshine State had begun to gain a foothold years earlier, at roughly the same time sweet Brooklyn had arrived at the Canidrome. Now, as Brooklyn was about to go home, the American struggle was reaching its denouement.

CHAPTER 12

NO SUNSHINE

"I hope that I have helped our greyhounds and made a little difference."

—Kathy Pelton

Tallahassee is a sleepy college town in the heart of the American Deep South, with wide roads flanked by live oak trees that weep Spanish moss. The air is thick and heavy, and eats away at buildings, leaving the city in a perpetual state of decay. It is surrounded by dense swamps, like the legendary Bradwell Bay, so remote that a visitor is much more likely to be bitten by a cottonmouth snake than to encounter another person. Those who live in this strange land are complicated, with an equal capacity for generosity and cruelty.

As the seat of government, Tallahassee serves as the stage for the annual meeting of the state legislature, occurring for two months in the late Winter to early Spring. Members of the Florida lobby corps congregate in a small chamber on the fourth floor of the capitol, directly between the House and Senate Chambers. There, an odd assortment of salesmen, lawyers, and political hacks crowd around television sets that offer live feeds of official proceedings. They preen for each other and slap backs, all while trying to hide their fear. This collection of wealth and power is incongruous with the surrounding poverty of much of Tallahassee—a disconnect that is emphasized in preposterous fashion on a special day each year when the lobbyists all report to the Capitol in seersucker suits.

A Florida law from 1992 limits lawmakers to serving eight-year terms. The statute was intended to encourage citizen involvement, but instead had the practical effect of strengthening the grip of special interests. So while elected officials come and go, paid lobbyists become institutions. A few of these power brokers are idolized like kings. They command six-figure fees from dozens of industries and immerse themselves in nearly every major deal struck by politicians. One of these mega lobbyists was a short man with thinning, slicked back hair named Ron Book. It was rumored that Ronnie owned more than a hundred $5,000 dollar suits and paid a small fortune to have them tailored every time he lost or gained weight. Another mogul was a tall, cocksure man named Brian Ballard. Brian had served as Chief of Staff to Governor Bob Martinez when he was only 26 and had gradually built an empire that included powerful clients like then-businessman Donald Trump.

All the major lobbyists had dog track clients. This made the pari-mutuels immensely powerful, nearly as consequential as Disney or "Big Sugar." Meanwhile, the greyhound breeders were represented by Jack Cory, a paunchy man with white hair and a thick New York accent. He wheeled a small suitcase around with him, as if prepared to fly home at any moment. Jack was a political pugilist with few ethical boundaries who presented a persistent thorn in the side of the track owners. In one infamous incident, an argument with Palm Beach Kennel Club owner Pat Rooney turned into a physical shoving match in one of the capitol building's washrooms.

By the time Carey arrived on the scene, Jack was in the twilight years of his career but still capable of some really dirty tricks. In an early committee hearing, he tried to discredit Carey by claiming he was a "terrorist." Instead of condemnation, his absurd claim elicited laughter from lawmakers and others present. Never one to learn from his mistakes and following the New Hampshire playbook, Jack then circulated a flier with a photo of Christine emblazoned with the words "animal rights lawyer." Jack did win one big round in those early days, though. He had an ally of his file a greyhound injury reporting bill ahead of us so that he could control and block its movement. Score one for the bad guys. (He would use that same trick years later by forming a political committee using the exact name we had intended to use for our local referendum. At least he was predictable!)

Over time, the Florida Greyhound. Association lobby team came to include three other lobbyists: Ramon Maury, former Lt. Governor Jeff Kottkamp, and retired judge Paul Hawkes. Maury was charismatic, but cynical. In one conversation, he admitted to Carey that he wouldn't let his own dog live in a racetrack kennel compound. He also claimed, quite blithely, that "there is no such thing as right or wrong." Hawkes was a former House member and District Court Judge, who had resigned after facing public criticism over his involvement in the construction of an extravagant $48 million courthouse featuring private kitchens for judges. Of the four, only Kottkamp garnered any respect from lawmakers.

Our first big Florida push occurred in the waning days of the 2010 session. Working alongside lobbyists for dog track owner Isadore "Izzy" Havenick, the son of industry icon Fred Havenick, we tried to amend gambling bills with language that repealed the state mandate for greyhound racing. This failed, but a foundation was laid for a more serious attempt the following year. Meanwhile, in the Fall, two game-changing events occurred. In October, a massive scandal erupted when more than three dozen greyhounds were found dead at Ebro Greyhound Park in northwest Florida. The dogs had been starved to death, with several more found in a state of near-death, their mouths and necks wrapped tightly with duct tape. Greyhound handler Ronnie Williams, who had abandoned his kennel after experiencing financial difficulties, was arrested on felony animal cruelty charges, and ultimately sentenced to five years in prison for his heinous acts. Shamelessly, his lawyers claimed that Williams had merely committed misdemeanor "acts of omission," and that this punishment was too severe.

A month later, we gained a crucial ally with the election of Republican Dana Young to the Florida House. Dana was sophisticated, passionate, and came from a well-known political family; her grandfather had been Senate President, and her uncle served in the State House of Representatives. Dana would later become House Majority Leader and serve in the Senate herself.

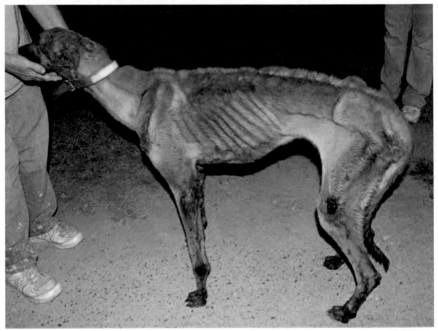

Starving dog found at kennel of Ronnie Williams, Ebro Greyhound Park, October 30, 2011 (State of Florida)

In 2011, Representative Young filed legislation to end the state mandate for live greyhound races. She worked day and night to find a compromise that was acceptable to all of the racetracks. Most of the license holders were ambivalent about her bill, but a few, like Flagler and Mardi Gras in South Florida, publicly supported it. As HB 1145 began to work its way through the process, a dysfunctional pattern emerged: Before each committee vote, dog track lobbyists would split into factions to scheme and attempt to double-cross each other. If even one track felt that another was getting a better deal, there would be no peace. The infighting would jeopardize the legislation until the very last moment, when the tracks would temporarily come together to ask for a yes vote in committee. But a moment later, the infighting would begin anew. With grit and a lot of hard work, Dana managed to navigate this minefield and pass her omnibus bill through both the House and Senate that Spring. All we needed now was for the two chambers to negotiate minor differences over track tax credits. Predictably, Palm Beach Kennel Club was angry that the House bill was less generous than the Senate's. On behalf of the Rooney family, Brian Ballard threatened to kill the legislation altogether unless the House accepted the more track-friendly version. In response, House leadership told the family to take it or leave it. The greyhounds needed a last-minute détente.

When the final day of the session came, Carey was racked with apprehension. With each passing hour, he could feel the opportunity to help thousands of dogs slipping away. Their fate was held by Palm Beach State Senator Maria Sachs, who had shepherded the measure through the upper chamber. Despite phone calls and emails from greyhound advocates across the state and around the world, she had decided to hold the bill unless the House accepted her version. Carey watched, late into the night, as a steady stream of frustrated allies begged Senator Sachs to relent. Alas, it was not to be. The Senate debated its final bill, and the gavel fell. The session was over, and Sachs never budged. Barely able to hold back tears, Carey saw Brian Ballard in the hall. "Don't worry, it will pass in the next two years," he said. Of course, this was just an empty promise. The greyhounds would not be given the justice they deserved for another decade, amounting to ten more years of suffering and death.

As the years passed, the Florida legislature became Carey's white whale. He spent two months each year living in Tallahassee, in a grand historic house just two blocks away from the capitol. Its windows were made of glass from the first territorial capitol building and it was filled from top to bottom with hidden historic artifacts of times gone by. The home also had its skeletons, such as the slave quarters hidden in the basement, just under the room where he stayed. Carey was often the only non-lawmaker in residence, giving him unique access to speak to members on a casual basis. He made friends with Cyndi Stevenson, a soft-spoken but shrewd Republican Representative from Jacksonville who was routinely underestimated by her colleagues. Carey would see Cyndi at the end of long days, and just as he had done with State Senator Tom Wilde two decades before, he would simply listen to her. Even though they had few conversations about greyhounds, it was Cyndi who later came to the rescue of our bill to ban the use of anabolic steroids at tracks. She sought Carey out to tell him that the Chairman of the Agriculture Committee was rounding up votes to defeat the bill. She pleaded with her colleagues privately and spoke for the dogs during the floor debate. She made sure the bill would pass, all without Carey ever asking for her help.

Although Carey grew to love North Florida, it was difficult for him to be away from home for so long. In his absence, Christine had to run the office, keep the house in order, and take care of the animals. Meanwhile, Carey experienced a deep loneliness. He took long solitary walks at night, listening to the sounds of frogs and cicadas in the dark. A few people tried to take care of him, including the brilliant ultra-distance runner Dana Stetson, a melancholy chess expert named Don Conner, and an older couple with rescued greyhounds, Bill and Elaine Swain. Dana showed Carey many of the hidden secrets of North Florida, including ancient Native American sites. Together, they went up the Wakulla River by canoe, where he saw enormous alligators. Once, a massive cottonmouth rose out of the water to threaten them. "Don't worry," Dana said, "It can't get in the boat. But watch the trees. They can fall into the boat from above." When Carey asked what to do in that case, Dana laughed and said, "jump out of the boat."

The greyhounds were also blessed to have lobbyist Marc Reichelderfer on their side. He was our secret weapon in Tallahassee because he usually knew what was about to happen and what we could do about it! While Marc and Carey tried to give the dogs a voice, Brian Ballard and Palm Beach took the position that no laws related to gambling could pass until the kennel club was allowed to have slot machines. This effectively suspended our bills. As before, the dogs were being held hostage by the businesses that made money off of them. Reflecting on this stalemate, Carey began to realize that the path forward wasn't through the legislature at all. The interests of the greyhounds would always be tied up, taken down, or simply sidelined by the many actors pushing their own separate agendas in Tallahassee. On the positive side, inaction by lawmakers had created a years-long opportunity to foster a massive public debate about the ethics of dog racing. Across the state, newspapers like the *Miami Herald*, *Florida New Times*, and the *Sarasota Herald-Tribune* published stories about the politics and problems of greyhound gambling. Reporters described the injuries and deaths suffered by racing greyhounds, the discovery of drugged dogs, and the lax regulations that allowed convicted criminals (including animal abusers) to work in the industry. Television stations interviewed lawmakers, track owners, greyhound advocates, and breeders. Multiple editorials were published against dog racing and in support of decoupling.

Public opinion was shifting, and people from all quarters of public life began to advocate for the dogs. Speech pathologist Kate MacFall spent all her free time volunteering at a local animal shelter in Tallahassee and would later serve as state director for the Humane Society of the United States. For years, she had been rescuing greyhounds from the broken-down kennels of the Jefferson County Kennel Club, a low-end track where many dogs died over the years. Every week, she brought a homeless dog to the state Cabinet meeting, where Attorney General Pam Bondi would make a televised pitch for adoption. Greyhounds became Kate's top priority, something AG Bondi came to share. Senator Maria Sachs spent years trying to pass greyhound decoupling after her initial hindrance, joined by State Senator Eleanor Sobel, a liberal icon who spent twenty-six years in the state legislature fighting for children and animals. In the House, Representative Jared Moskowitz fought for the greyhounds session after session, trying everything he could to help them. In 2016, the greyhounds gained another hero with the election of Carlos Guillermo Smith from Orlando, the first openly gay member of the Florida Legislature. From the right, the mission was picked up by Senate President Don Gaetz, his son and future Congressman Matt Gaetz, Republican Party campaign guru Joel Springer, and former Senate President Tom Lee, among others. This was an odd coalition that brought together people who didn't agree on anything—ever! The one thing they all agreed on was that greyhound racing was cruel and needed to end.

Tony Glover, a former Director of the agency that regulated greyhound racing, was the last person to join the greyhound team. A thoughtful lawyer who truly believed in justice, he was the first person of color to serve as director of the Division of Pari-Mutuel Wagering. But he had stepped down as chief racing regulator after dealing firsthand with the unrelenting corruption of the greyhound breeders and kennel operators. Under his leadership, the agency issued multiple fines after discovering that greyhounds were testing positive for drugs all across the state. But the dogmen and women pushed back by shamelessly suing to nullify the very rules he was using to punish them! Such was the level of their depravity. When Tony began working with Christine and Carey, these same folks spread rumors that Tony was a drug dealer who had manipulated greyhound urine samples with his own stash. Although he never said it out loud, we could all see the obvious racist aspect to these attacks.

The Division of Pari-mutuel Wagering had also made its own mistakes, one of which was granting special waivers to dangerous felons, allowing them to work in the industry. In the most egregious case, clemency had been given to a man named Saul Mays, who operated out of the Jefferson County Kennel Club in Monticello, Florida. In 1988, Mays had been convicted of felony kidnapping and aggravated battery charges for sexually assaulting his estranged wife at gunpoint. In fact, Mays had been arrested at least ten other times for driving while intoxicated, larceny, fraud, criminal mischief, and domestic violence. He was the poster child for the overturn of the felony waiver program. In 2010, we called for a formal investigation of Mays after hearing from a confidential informant that greyhounds were regularly removed from Mays' kennels, taken off-site, and killed. Officials took no action. A separate state investigation had also revealed that many of Mays' active dogs were housed under terrible conditions, underfed or starving, and even jaundiced from tick fever. Still, the state took no action. Thankfully, the bad publicity which ensued led the Florida Greyhound Association to submit its own neglect complaint two years later. Unfortunately, justice was still not served, since this only resulted in a measly $200 fine for Mays.

After several years of lobbying in 2013, we did manage to convince the Division of Pari-Mutuel Wagering to adopt the first ever greyhound welfare rules, which included a key requirement that deaths be reported to the public. This provision was a victory, even if flawed. Under its narrow language, only deaths that occurred on racetrack property, including the kennel compound, had to be reported. If a dog were taken away and killed, the death would escape disclosure. But even with this limitation, the new death notifications proved that a greyhound was dying, on average, every three days at a Florida racetrack. Each month, we received new reports, and they were heartbreaking. One of these notifications was for a dog named PorPorPitifullMe. She had been born on May 20, 2013, and trucked to the Palm Beach Kennel Club when she was just 18 months old. On November 18, 2014, PorPorPitifullMe was entered to race for the eighth time. According to the state record, the lure malfunctioned, she "attempted to jump the rail," and was electrocuted. Deaths like this had been occurring for decades, but for the first time, the public could know about them.

Greyhound decoupling was hotly debated in 2012 and 2013, but we could not overcome all of the obstacles preventing its passage. Both years, we advanced far into the process, and were alive and fighting until the very last days of session. In the end, our efforts again collapsed amidst infighting among the myriad of gambling interests. It became clear that the political parties were using gambling as a fundraising mechanism, keeping the issue alive as a way to obtain continuing campaign contributions. But even while track owners tried to convince politicians to give them more gambling rights and the contributions kept flowing, our anti-racing movement continued to slowly advance. Carey was now playing a different game, beyond the chess board. This gave our fight new life while also leading to some laughable anecdotes. For example, one day a peculiar lawmaker named John Tobia called Carey into his office. He said he absolutely hated dogs but voted with us because it made his daughter believe him to be a better person than he really was! This was a strange encounter and spoke to the quirkiness of Tobia, but also underscored the political capital we were able to build simply by being present and genuine.

While Carey and Marc fought in Tallahassee, a large grassroots movement began to take shape. The self-appointed leader was South Florida activist Kathy Pelton. She was model-tall and thin, blond, with a sharp mind and a steely gaze that could be both reassuring and intimidating. For years, she had operated an insurance business with her husband Ken, who was her best friend and confidant. In their retirement, they had discovered animal advocacy, become vegan, and adopted several greyhounds, including two charming dogs named Jack and Jill. Kathy had strong bonds with the people close to her, including her children and grandchildren, but the greyhound fight consumed her. She hosted tables at community events, canvassed door-to-door, and set up meetings with lawmakers and candidates running for office. Kathy commanded respect from everyone she met, and even forged a relationship of sorts with cantankerous dog track representative Danny Adkins, whom she spoke to every year during an annual protest she held outside his racetrack. During our decades-long Florida fight, Kathy was omnipresent, working around the clock, all the while brimming with optimism that the greyhounds would be set free.

Kathy and her team had a huge impact on the debate in 2013. At a strategy session before a South Florida gambling hearing, Carey laid out a detailed plan about how to best pitch greyhound decoupling. In passing, he mentioned a second issue he thought was less important: greyhound injury reporting. We had fought for the reporting of injuries as part of the state welfare rules, alongside death reporting, but had lost. The activists listened, and then ignored Carey's advice completely. In the hearing, one person after another pleaded for lawmakers to make greyhound injuries public, while almost no one mentioned decoupling. Florida was one of only two states, they argued, where greyhound injuries were kept hidden from public view. The other state was Alabama—and who wanted to be lumped in with that state, they said! This hit home with lawmakers, including Senator Eleanor Sobel. Before the night was over, she told Carey that she wanted to file a greyhound injury reporting bill. Just like that, injury reporting had chosen itself as the next step.

Florida woman protests dog racing, November 1, 2014
(Kinfay Moroti/© news-press.com-USA Today Network)

The following Spring, Senator Sobel introduced a bill to require greyhound injury reports. She cleverly named it after Victoria Gaetz, wife of Senate President Don Gaetz, who was an unflagging animal rights supporter herself. With the Senate President's blessing, the Sobel bill comfortably passed through two committees, and was approved by the full Senate on a vote of forty to zero. This turned out to be a pyrrhic victory, though, when the House refused to even consider the proposal. Over the next few years, we proved ourselves capable of passing injury reporting in one chamber or the other, but could never succeed in getting a bill to the Governor's desk. We even passed a budget proviso, with Senator Tom Lee's help, to require the Division to adopt injury reporting as a regulation. But the agency simply ignored the mandate.

Always looking for new moves to make, Carey recommended that Christine draft language to bring a local ballot question to the voters of Seminole County, where the iconic Sanford Orlando dog track was located. Seminole was a county governed by home rule petition, which allowed it to have greater self-determination than some other counties with dog tracks. It also offered six months for signature collection with a relatively low number of signatures needed for qualification. So in late 2015, we created the Committee to Protect Greyhounds.

In the months that followed, volunteers led by Carla and Bryan Wilson of Winter Springs began working to collect the 14,000 signatures required for a place on the next ballot. The Greyhound Protection Act of Seminole County would achieve three key things: require the track to license individual greyhounds for the first time, make injury and death records available to the public, and open up all racing kennels to regular inspection. The idea was simple, to require that greyhounds be treated like all other dogs in the jurisdiction. After the signatures were successfully collected, County attorney A. Bryant Applegate attempted to shut us down by circulating a legal memo claiming that keeping records for greyhounds wasn't necessary and that, even if it were, the proposed ordinance was preempted by the state's racing laws. Christine argued that the county had a right—and in fact, a duty, as part of its overall animal protection powers—to ensure the safety of over one thousand greyhounds in the jurisdiction. She also pointed out that the track was already keeping injury and death records, so allowing such reports to be shared publicly created no extra burden. To her delight, the Board of County Commissioners not only decided to ignore Mr. Applegate, but took up the language of our initiative and passed it themselves on August 10, 2016. We were thrilled with this happy outcome, as were all the volunteers who had worked so hard to collect signatures, host information tables, and help us deal with an obstreperous County Division of Elections. Every time we heard "no," the greyhounds told us to say yes. And that's what we did! This positive spirit inspired our entire effort and set the stage for the bigger battles to come.

After the Orlando measure passed, greyhound breeders tried to strike back in court. They hired former Lt. Governor Jeff Kottkamp to file suit against the County, hoping to block the measure from going into effect. They lost, which also turned out to be shades of things to come.

Meanwhile, greyhound drugging issues took center stage in Tallahassee when Representative Carlos Guillermo Smith filed a bill to outlaw the use of anabolic steroids in greyhounds. All female racing dogs were routinely given methyltestosterone, a banned substance that builds muscles. The drug also interrupted their natural cycle and prevented loss of race days. Although we had not yet won on injury reporting, we felt ready to fight for both reforms simultaneously. The Smith bill was also a trap for the industry, an invitation to defend its reckless steroid use. The practice had been outlawed in greyhound racing jurisdictions overseas, and veterinary sources like the *Merck Veterinary Manual* discouraged it. Just as in Tucson years before, the industry didn't have a leg to stand on. But this was a recalcitrant bunch, unwilling to improve or change as long as money could be made from inhumane shortcuts. Jack Cory and the greyhound breeders defended their practice as an innocuous form of "doggy birth control." After a tremendous amount of work and successful passage through several committees, the steroids bill passed the House—but we still couldn't manage to get it through the Senate. Not giving up, we tried to ban steroids again the following year. While that effort eventually failed as well, we could feel that our reform agenda was gaining ground. Sometimes when you lose, you really win!

Meanwhile, the greyhound drug issue gained even more steam in the Summer of 2017, when a dozen greyhounds under the control of trainer Charles McClellan tested positive for cocaine. The dogs were in a kennel owned by Steve Sarras at Orange Park in Jacksonville. The positives were first reported locally by *First Coast*

News, and then covered by media around the state. One dog, WW's Flicka, tested positive for cocaine repeatedly, and ran the fastest time of her career in one of the races in which she tested positive. Flicka was already four years old in this race, beyond her athletic peak. Regulator Tony Glover was alarmed by the facts of the case and revoked McClellan's license altogether, along with the license of a second trainer. The two then hired lawyers to challenge the entire drug testing program itself. Unbelievably, McClellan and the others implicated eventually escaped punishment by successfully claiming they had no notice of the changes in testing methodologies, so they could not be enforced against them. But what kennel operators did not understand was that this reprieve would only provide further evidence that dog racing was unsavory. In the end, the industry paid a heavy price for the dismissal, with many reporters covering the case as an attack on the very system that was supposed to keep dog racing clean.

During this period Carey unsuccessfully tried to negotiate with the dogmen and find common ground. In the spring of 2017, Carey approached Florida Greyhound Association lobbyist Paul Hawkes. He urged him to accept our bill to outlaw the use of anabolic steroids and use its passage as proof that the industry was capable of reform. The FGA lobby team simply ignored his entreaty. A few months later, in June of 2017, Carey was invited to speak at a conference hosted by the National Council of Legislators from Gaming States. When the NGA learned of the invitation it complained to organizers and secured a speaking slot on the same panel. Undaunted, Carey gave a presentation in which he contrasted the divergent way in which the greyhound and horse industries had reacted to the challenges facing them. He highlighted the open debate in horse racing on drug abuse and compared this transparency to the secrecy and obstruction of greyhound breeders. Carey even included polling numbers which showed that 81% of voters were troubled by greyhound confinement, 80% of voters were concerned about greyhound injuries, and 76% of voters were more likely to support an end of dog racing because of the use of anabolic steroids. NGA Executive Secretary Jim Gartland followed Carey, and rather than respond, repeated the same talking points and denials the industry had been using for years. Afterwards, Carey invited Gartland to speak with him privately. Gartland assented, but then failed to show for the meeting.

In December of 2017, GREY2K USA Worldwide released a report on drugs in the greyhound racing industry, entitled *No Confidence: Drugs in the American Greyhound Racing Industry*. Principally the work of Research Director Matt Read, this white paper included documentation of 847 greyhound drug positives over a decade, including 71 cocaine positives. The report also addressed the use of anabolic steroids, the lack of funding for greyhound drug testing, industry attacks on drug testing programs, and the insufficient penalties for drug positives. In one case, a greyhound trainer in Alabama had received a paltry $50 fine for having a greyhound test positive for cocaine. In another troubling incident, the Texas Racing Commission admitted that it had significantly reduced drug testing at Gulf Greyhound Park in 2011 after the track requested a "reevaluation" of the testing program. Carey and Christine barnstormed the country to release the report, meeting with newspaper editorial boards, allied groups, and lawmakers.

As one year led into another, Kathy Pelton quietly continued her grassroots work but also joined our board of directors. She was intimately involved in almost every aspect of the Florida fight and kept working even as she faced considerable obstacles. When a greyhound Kathy had adopted, named Eddy, was diagnosed with bone cancer in 2009, it only made her work harder. Two years later, another greyhound she adopted, named Honey, died unexpectedly. Kathy kept working. Years later, when Kathy was herself diagnosed with cancer, and her husband Ken also faced perilous health issues, she kept working. By the summer of 2017, Kathy was quite ill. Undaunted, she insisted on meeting with House members who had voted against outlawing steroids. Ignoring Carey's warnings that this was a pointless exercise, Kathy was determined to meet with these wayward members, especially the ones that lived in her South Florida area. For weeks, her meeting requests went ignored, until eventually one member, State Representative Kionne McGhee, agreed to see her. In this meeting, Kathy told Representative McGhee, who was a close ally of Jack Cory, that she had cancer and would soon travel to the great beyond. Kathy told McGhee that she knew he would get another chance to vote on the steroids bill, and wanted a personal promise from her that he would vote yes. McGhee was deeply moved, and kept his word the following Spring. Shortly after the third incarnation of our steroid bill was filed, he reached out to Representative Guillermo Smith and not only said he would vote in favor, but asked what he could do to help move the bill along.

On September 29, Kathy gave Carey and Christine an update on a presentation she had given to a middle school class the day before. She was disappointed that they had only given her fifteen minutes and had not allowed her greyhounds Jack and Jill to participate. She said her cancer had returned, and that she would be looking over us to make sure the greyhounds won. A week later, Kathy left our world the day before her 74th birthday. Ken was inconsolable, and waves of grief reverberated throughout the animal welfare community. Hundreds of people attended the Celebration of Her Life, a joyous event that left everyone with a sense of love and gratitude.

The same week Kathy passed, Carey received an unexpected phone call from Joel Springer. Joel was a close advisor of former Senate President Tom Lee, and responsible for running Senate campaigns for the Republican Party of Florida. He was fiercely independent, conservative, and had rescued a series of dogs including a pointer named Norman, whom he loved dearly. Joel said that Senator Lee had been appointed to the Constitutional Revision Commission, a unique panel that met in Florida every twenty years and had the ability to bypass the legislature and propose constitutional amendments directly to the voters. The two met for coffee, and when Carey asked what this had to do with dogs, Joel looked him in the eye. "President Lee is interested in giving voters a chance to completely outlaw greyhound racing."

CHAPTER 13

THE LANDSLIDE

"Take away the arguments against Amendment 13, and voters are faced with a fundamental truth: Dog racing's day has passed and far too many animals are being abused. It's time for Florida to close the books."

—Ocala Star Banner Editorial, October 26, 2018

Shortly after moving to Loxahatchee, Florida, Sonia Stratemann decided to adopt a greyhound. She had recently relocated to the Sunshine State with her husband and three young children, and had lost her beloved white and brown lurcher, Jackson, after the move. Sonia had rescued Jackson many years earlier, when his mother had been discovered pregnant and abandoned in a California date field. Many lurchers are part greyhound, and long-legged Jackson was unlike any dog she had ever met. Heartbroken, Sonia called her local dog track, the Palm Beach Kennel Club, hoping to adopt. When she didn't receive a response, she phoned repeatedly until her persistence was rewarded with an invitation to the track kennels. Upon arrival at the compound—a jumble of rickety shanties surrounded by overgrown bushes, a guard shack, and a barbed wire fence, Sonia was shown dogs that had been rejected by adoption groups. Some dogs had been abandoned because they were intensely shy. This is so common in the racing world that there is a name for them: spooks. They sit paralyzed in their cages, afraid of the entire world. Other dogs she saw had serious wounds or fractures that no one wanted to pay to fix. The saddest of all were the greyhounds that had been forsaken simply because their coat was black, which some believed made them harder to place into homes. Among these innocent faces was a four-year-old black brindle boy named Leroy, who was recovering from an injured back. Sonia took him home immediately. Within a few months, the Stratemann family had taken in five more greyhounds.

Sonia founded Elite Greyhound Adoptions, and over time, earned the respect of both the industry and the community at large. She met many greyhound trainers, and some became trusted friends. Elite was named the official adoption program for the Palm Beach track, which gave Sonia regular access to the kennel compound and an endless supply of dogs to rescue. This was a Faustian bargain and meant she could not be openly critical of the racing industry. Sonia tried to overlook the sad conditions at the kennels, but could not help but wonder how this track could bill itself as the "most glamorous in the world." Certainly, there was no glamor for the greyhounds. So she focused on helping as many dogs as she could. Elite became known as the group that would take dogs with broken legs, and eventually she helped adopt out more than two thousand spent ex-racers. Along the way, Sonia privately informed track executives about the cases of serious abuse she witnessed, all of which they either ignored or, worse, simply covered up.

Then, tragedy struck. In February of 2017, Sonia's life was torn apart when her seventeen-year-old son, Donovan, passed away unexpectedly in a senseless accident. Donovan was a compassionate young man who had a gift when it came to helping animals. This disaster plunged the family into an impenetrable grief, a darkness that threatened to consume them. After many months, a tiny ray of light broke through this shadow when Sonia heard the news that Senator Tom Lee had filed a CRC proposal to end greyhound racing. Here was something Donovan would have embraced. She reached out to Carey through people she knew in the rescue community, and told him that she was ready to tell her story. She wanted to open up about all the greyhound cruelty she had witnessed in hopes of making a difference. The industry feared Sonia, because she was an intimate of the racing world, and could speak with direct knowledge.

On the day Tom Lee's proposal was given its first hearing before the Constitution Revision Commission, Sonia met Carey there. She had hardly slept the night before, spoken to Donovan during the long drive to Tallahassee, and arrived terrified. Meanwhile, Carey was completely convinced we were about to lose the vote. They were joined by other greyhound advocates including longtime volunteers Bryan and Carla Wilson, Kate MacFall, and Tampa greyhound rescuer Don Goldstein. Don was a retired Coast Guard officer, and brought a rescued greyhound named Mira with him. Mira exemplified industry overbreeding, as her Hall of Fame father had sired more than eleven thousand dogs for racing.

One by one, advocates implored committee members to support the greyhound proposal. The final speaker was Ken Pelton, who told commissioners he was there because his wife Kathy couldn't be. He described how much he loved his recently departed partner, and how hard she had fought to help the dogs. When Ken was finished, silence fell over the room as many of us held back tears. Attention then turned to Chair Jacqui Thurlow-Lippisch, a committed environmentalist who had served as Mayor of tiny Sewall's Point in southeast Florida. In an unusual move, she asked for Mira to be brought up next to her on the dais for the vote. One by one, commissioners began to speak and announced they would be voting yes. To our amazement, it appeared the Lee proposal might actually pass its first committee! When Chair Thurlow-Lippisch asked for a roll call, it was adopted unanimously. Elation erupted throughout the room, as Commissioners took selfies with Mira. After so many years of struggle in Florida, here was a small, splendid glimpse of justice. Although there was still a long road ahead, this was the first moment advocates dared to imagine that the greyhounds might actually reach the ballot.

Joyce Carta describes the life and death of a racing greyhound before the Florida
Constitution Revision Commission, St. Petersburg, March 13, 2018
(John Sokolinski)

Over the next few months, we slowly advanced through the CRC. There was a total of seven hearings held all across the state. Hundreds of greyhound advocates came in support, many wearing their GREY2K USA t-shirts and buttons. We armed our speakers with large, full color photos of dogs who had died racing and each volunteer held up a photo and read a different dog's story to the Commissioners. At the very last meeting, which took place in St. Petersburg on March 13, 2018, Christine submitted a petition with 250,000 signatures in support of the measure. She also dismantled the latest false claims that ending dog racing would somehow unconstitutionally "take" the private property of our opponents. Afterward, she was met with extreme animosity from the greyhound breeders in attendance who hissed and cursed as she walked by. At one of the earlier CRC hearings, Carey had personally approached Florida Greyhound Association President Jim Blanchard and openly offered to negotiate. In response, a crowd of angry greyhound trainers shouted him down with insults and threats. Apparently, there would be no negotiating! While the Florida folks were less savvy than our original opponent, George Carney of Massachusetts, they had the same irrational confidence.

Meanwhile, Carey learned that Attorney General Pam Bondi had taken an interest in our fight. In addition to being a member of the CRC Commission, Bondi was a rising star in the Republican Party. Along with Lara Trump, Bondi would turn out to be a critical ally. Together, these two strong conservative women fought tooth and nail to make sure we had the necessary support. The team grew again when the Humane Society of the United State hired lobbyist Rich Heffley, who was both smart and hard-working. Just as Michael Preston Green had been critical to our victory in Arizona, Rich helped us navigate a complicated and politically treacherous path. Attorney Len Collins, then with the firm Nelson Mullins, provided critical guidance, as did our lobbyist Marc Reichelderfer.

On a hot April afternoon, the greyhound proposal came up for its final vote in the CRC. This was the absolute, final hurdle that was standing between us and the voters—the stakes could not have been higher. That's why greyhound breeders flooded the Capitol, wearing matching white t-shirts with red letters demanding a No vote. Some came with dogs but were not allowed into the chamber. Sadly, others brought their children, who sat and listened to Pam Bondi passionately describe the many cruelties of dog racing. What they did not know is that, overnight, Governor Rick Scott himself had been lobbying members on our behalf. Finally, the moment arrived. Like dreamers, we watched Commissioners passionately argue over dog racing, just as Sheila Roberge and Lou D'Allesandro had done a decade earlier on the floor of the New Hampshire Senate. Tom Lee urged his colleagues to vote for common sense, while former Senator Chris Smith blasted the proposal, claiming it would cost jobs and somehow be a backdoor to expanded gambling. Time stood still as the gavel fell. In a flash, the vote board lit up. YES: 27. NO: 10. It had happened! After so many generations of dogs dying at Florida tracks, voters would now decide the fate of commercial greyhound racing in its biggest and most historic state. We were designated to appear last on the ballot as Amendment 13, which we hoped would bring the good luck the greyhounds needed.

With the election now only six short months away, there was no time to waste. Joined by the Humane Society of the United States and the Doris Day Animal League, we formed a political committee called the Committee to Protect Dogs. The effort gained another benefactor when Animal Wellness Action joined as a top contributor. AWA was a new organization, formed by Wayne Pacelle after he was forced to leave the Humane Society in the wake of harassment allegations. Wayne's departure had split the animal protection community apart, creating a deep and painful rift.

Carey wrote a comprehensive strategy memo that broke the campaign down into seven phases, focusing on themes such as grassroots support, greyhound drug positives, and confinement. He believed that winning campaigns are the ones which find a simple message and deliver it with one powerful voice. This was our goal. As part of this strategy, and given that the election was so close upon us, Carey strongly recommended that we waste no money on lawn signs or buttons but rather use all the resources we could muster for TV ads. It took great discipline, but we stayed true to the plan. Our only paid worker was Carla Wilson, who served as the statewide grassroots coordinator and spokesperson. In the end, we spent more than 98% of all funds raised on the broadcast campaign.

As we executed this carefully conceived plan of attack, the industry was in crisis. Dissatisfied with the Florida Greyhound Association, a group of greyhound breeders and trainers formed a competing political group called the "Committee to Support Greyhounds." This moniker was an obvious attempt to confuse voters and followed the playbook of the losing "Massachusetts Animal Interest Coalition" from years before. The CSG, as its supporters came to refer to it, was chaired by a former kennel worker from Texas named Jennifer Newcome. Rather than wage a disciplined campaign and deliver a single, clear message, CSG spent money on anything and everything including billboards, lawn signs, and cable television ads. They raised so little—just over $100,000—and spent it in such a diffuse way that they had zero impact.

Meanwhile, the Florida Greyhound Association focused itself on a forlorn legal strategy. In a desperate attempt to prevent a vote on Amendment 13, the group hired former Supreme Court Justice Major Harding, and filed a lawsuit to strike the greyhounds from the ballot. Harding had an existing relationship with Jeff Kottkamp, whom he had defended against accusations of ethics violations years before. We knew this latest lawsuit was a longshot, but we didn't want to take any chances. We hired a powerful legal team, led by Stephen Turner, who defended our position alongside the state Attorney General's office. We were confident we would prevail, and our main source of concern was the particular jurist the case had been assigned to, Judge Karen Gievers. Gievers was nearing the mandatory retirement age, and several of her recent rulings had been overturned in high-profile cases.

Judge Gievers was conspicuously hostile at the hearing, and a few weeks later, our worst fears were realized when she issued a blunt decision that not only struck down Amendment 13, but claimed it was a form of what she termed "trickeration." This was the worst-case scenario. Even though we were optimistic her ruling would eventually be overturned, it threw everything into disarray. For five long weeks, we endured a blizzard of negative news stories that all but declared our greyhound amendment dead in the water. We kept our heads up, were forthright with volunteers, and simply kept working. The grassroots team continued unabated, and all over the state, volunteers educated voters at local fairs, town gatherings, dog parks, and neighborhood events.

Thankfully, even while this storm raged around us, our opponents continued to make mistakes. While monitoring the "No on 13" Facebook page, we noticed that a man named Jesse James Hodges had been added to the group as an official member. He had posted a message of solidarity with greyhound breeders, saying he "come(s) as a friend" to help fight the animal activists. Several dog racing supporters responded to his plea, with one thanking Hodges and calling him a "hound brother." When we took a closer look at Hodges, bright red flags popped up everywhere. His profile photo depicted two young puppies with a severed pig head, and we learned he had been charged with twelve counts of animal cruelty in Louisiana only months earlier. We publicly called on "No on 13" to disavow his support, pointing out that their campaign had become a safe haven for accused animal abusers. The Hodges story was reported by *Politico Florida*, and the industry did eventually distance itself from him. But it was too little too late. The damage had already been done.

Dog racers also rallied around a central Florida artist and agitator named Jeff Sonksen, a mostly unemployed painter who had become known in the community for placing graffiti-like images on public fencing. Sonksen visited the Sanford Orlando Kennel Compound regularly and produced a series of industry propaganda videos. A fringe personality who loved the limelight, the erstwhile artist was both aggressive and bellicose, yet clownish, and ironically this turned out to give our campaign a great advantage. As election day approached, his GoPro segments at track kennels across the state became more frequent and increasingly unhinged. He had a cozy relationship with a White Nationalist named Eric Wilson, who used a confederate flag as his Facebook profile photo and promoted predictions of a "New Waco." In one exchange, Wilson referred to Sonksen as "my boy" and "brother," and bragged that he had defended Sonksen against animal advocates, whom he referred to as "thieving . . . pathetic liars." In response, Sonksen thanked Wilson. These incidents underscored a general lack of decency that permeated the "No on 13" team. This odious tone started at the top, and seeped through the entire group. In the years since Amendment 13, Sonksen has largely disappeared but maintains his reputation as anti-animal by regularly confronting PETA activists at SeaWorld.

In late August, the Florida Supreme Court heard oral arguments in the Gievers case. The Justices questioned Major Harding thoroughly, perhaps in an effort to help his presentation. In response, he answered with wild accusations and, at one point, began reading the US Constitution. By contrast, the state's attorney Deputy Solicitor Jordan E. Pratt was organized, succinct, and eloquent. He knew the facts and the law better than anyone else in the courtroom and had worked very hard to protect the proposed amendment. Days later, the Court issued a forceful 6-1 ruling that overturned the lower court and confirmed Amendment 13's rightful place on the ballot. The Court also refuted a set of scare tactics and false claims that the FGA had been making, including the canard that the Amendment would expand gambling. In hindsight, this industry lawsuit turned out to be a blessing. It distracted the industry, wasted opponents' resources, and gave advocates a Supreme Court ruling that directly refuted many of the false claims greyhound racers had been spewing. Once again, an apparent setback had turned out to be a blessing in disguise.

But the fight wasn't yet over, and it seemed like the industry's dirty tricks would never stop. For example, as election day neared, dog racers began to enforce a "blacklist" of outspoken greyhound adoption groups. This draconian action had been threatened for years, going all the way back to 2013, when the Iowa Greyhound Association published a flier that warned adopters the greyhound breed would disappear if they didn't defend the industry.

> Look at your pet. Now look ahead to the future and your current pet is gone. You want another greyhound. You also loved to buy your heart hound collars for the holidays, a nice bed and a comfy coat . . . Now it is all over. The tracks are gone . . . the farms are gone. All the adoption groups are gone . . . This is reality. This IS the way it will be if YOU make bad choices. Don't be a sheep . . . do not adopt from groups who are against the industry.

While this had mostly been an idle threat in the past, the industry was now faced with an existential threat. Access to dogs was not only cut off to groups that were against racing, but also to organizations that were neutral. Greyhound Pets of America, the largest industry-funded group in the country, amended its bylaws to explicitly support commercial greyhound racing. The NGA created a list of "approved" adoption groups that the FGA enforced. To make the cut, groups were required to "dispel the myths" about dog racing, and "not make false or negative statements about the racing industry." Such groups also had to refuse funding from animal protection groups, including GREY2K USA Worldwide. Through this corrupt process, the compassionate and wonderful greyhound rescue community which we had supported for many years was decimated. In its place, a closed network of pro racing groups began serving as public relations props for the industry. The irony is that the people behind these groups knew more about the cruelty of dog racing than any greyhound advocate on the other side.

Some groups took the industry decree to yet another level, only adopting dogs to people who demonstrated that they were pro-racing. The issue was so weaponized that adoption group board members resigned, and friendships ended over the deal that had been made with racing interests. The industry believed that coercing adoption groups would save it, but in the end, the gambit had no impact. Not enough voters heard from these pro-racing adoption agencies to make a difference, and those who did were confused. It made no sense that people who cared about greyhounds would support racing, and folks were rightly skeptical about their motivations.

At the same time, dog racers accused "Yes on 13" of "not having a plan" for the departure of greyhounds when Amendment 13 passed. This was Massachusetts all over again! In reality, Carey and Christine were proud of the many ways GREY2K USA Worldwide had supported greyhound adoption over the years. Christine had led successful programs to find homes for all displaced dogs when greyhound racing had ended in Arizona in 2016 and again at the Canidrome in 2018. Our US-based "Greyhounds First Coalition" was succeeded by the international "Macau Airlift." We had raised and granted hundreds of thousands in direct funding to adoption groups, and regularly encouraged supporters to adopt a greyhound in need. We have always believed that adoption efforts should be non-political, and that all sides should put the dogs first.

While the industry was busy strong-arming the greyhound rescue community, we focused on building a grassroots network and raising funds. The campaign received a massive boost in late July when the Doris Day Animal Foundation gave a jaw-dropping donation of $1.5 million. Doris Day was not only a beloved actress and singer, but had started her work in animal advocacy by helping greyhounds and horses. She had founded Spay Day USA, testified repeatedly before Congress on animal issues, and made a massive impact through the several nonprofits she formed. Her gift was a seminal moment for the dogs and would not have happened without the support of Sara Amundson, who had served as chief executive of the Doris Day Animal League and an early GREY2K

USA Board Member. With funding in hand, Deno and Jeorge Seder began to craft our television ads, using footage of greyhound confinement that had been proudly released on social media by Jeff Sonksen. It turned out that allying themselves with "Paint the Trail" filmmaker Sonksen amounted to yet another self-inflicted wound for the greyhound breeders. The same mistake that had been made in Massachusetts when greyhound breeders had released images and video from inside their kennels. Everything old was new again.

State Senator Dana Young with Protect Dogs/Yes on 13 volunteers, Humane Society of Tampa Bay, June 14, 2018 (Christine A. Dorchak/GREY2K USA Worldwide)

Having initially focused fundraising dollars on paying lawyers to bring the failed legal challenge, the Florida Greyhound Association ultimately raised a total of just over $400,000, most of which was used to wage a campaign of disinformation that would have made Roy Cohn proud. Greyhound breeders bought Facebook ads that didn't mention greyhound racing at all, but instead claimed that

Amendment 13 would ban other activities, like hunting and sports fishing. In a hurricane of lies, the FGA claimed Amendment 13 would in fact expand gambling, ban amateur dog events, and even cause the death of thousands of greyhounds who would be rendered "jobless." This last distortion was particularly galling, and ignored the fact that the ballot question included a 26-month wind down period to allow for the organized release of dogs from closing racetracks. The crooked campaign reached a nadir a few weeks before election day when Jack Cory stood on a South Florida debate stage and repeatedly mocked Sonia Stratemann over the death of her son Donovan. This insensitivity won no allies or converts to his cause.

From one end of the state to the other, "Yes on 13" began to pick up more and more endorsements, including from nine newspapers with dog tracks in their local communities. These newspapers knew the issue well, and had spent years reporting on greyhound deaths, cocaine positives, and an endless cycle of industry scandals. By election day, the greyhounds had received nods from a diverse group of community leaders, including democratic gubernatorial candidate Andrew Gillum, Mike Huckabee, the League of Women Voters of Florida, the Florida Federation of Republican Women, and the Democratic Progressive Caucus of Florida. The campaign was bursting with support.

With only days left, Christine scrambled to raise more money for television. By this point, we were confident we would get a majority vote, but we still needed a 60% supermajority for the Amendment to pass. This was an incredibly high hurdle! We doubled down on the TV ad buy everywhere we could and added the Pensacola market at the last minute. We knew that if enough voters heard the "Yes on 13" message, the greyhounds would win. This turned out to be correct, but the cost was crippling. We spent nearly a million dollars in the Miami media market alone, and hundreds of thousands in other markets including Orlando, West Palm Beach, Ft. Myers, Jacksonville, and Tampa. Our ads went on the air on October 15, and aired morning, noon, and night.

The day before the election, the entire office team flew down to South Florida. After a sleepless night, we reported to one of the Palm Beach voting locations as soon as it opened. It was hot, and most voters were not interested in conversation. They just wanted to cast their ballots and get back home. Hours passed. In the late afternoon, Carey received word that a newspaper in Southwest Florida had been conducting an exit survey with actual voters leaving the polls in a deeply conservative district. To our amazement, Amendment 13 seemed to be passing by a huge margin, performing even better than Republican gubernatorial candidate Ron DeSantis. If the exit polls were accurate we weren't just going to win, we were going to win *BIG*! As dusk fell, we bundled into a crowded Lyft, with people sitting on each other's laps, and made our way to a watch party.

The clock struck seven, the polls closed, and we all froze in our seats. No one could breathe. Carey's phone rang and we had the first returns, showing Amendment 13 passing all over the state by massive margins, 65%, 69%, 73% . . . Could we really have won? We arrived at the party, and the returns were real. The greyhounds were coming in above 60% everywhere, and within moments Carey had powered up Christine's laptop, pulled up a press statement declaring victory, and hit send. Christine found a spot in a back room and wrote our most important broadcast email ever, announcing to the world of greyhound advocates that dog racing would soon end in its biggest state! By the next morning, it was clear that we had not only prevailed, we had won by a massive landslide vote of 69% to 31%. Everything we had done had been right, and Carey's theory of the campaign had been vindicated. We felt like we were living through history, and the years of work that it took to reach this moment really came home to us. It was a weighty moment, and we cherished this second opportunity to celebrate a clear vote for the greyhounds, this time delivered by millions of compassionate Floridians.

Dog racing proponents were utterly struck by the voters' decision as well, but in a completely different way. Even months later, NGA executive Jim Gartland found himself in disbelief. "What happened?" Gartland asked in *The Greyhound Review*. "There is no real answer to that question," he wrote in the industry magazine. "There is much speculation and some would like to say a lot of blame, one way or another, but in the end, it looks like the industry wasn't able overcome [sic] fighting a massively funded campaign by anti-racing groups." Gartland went on to suggest that perhaps the election had been rigged. The response from the dog track owners themselves was not what we expected at all. Miami track owner Izzy Havenick, who had been a reliable ally in the decoupling fight, told a local newspaper he had fully expected Amendment 13 to *fail*. By contrast, dog track executive Dan Adkins, who did nothing to help, happily took credit for the victory. Industry-affiliated adoption groups simply refused to talk to the press at all.

In the end, Amendment 13 passed for a very simple reason: Floridians love dogs, and they decided that no more greyhounds should die so that people could gamble on them. In a strange and wondrous land, voters aligned with their better selves, and gave gentle hounds the freedom they had been denied for 87 long years.

Chapter 14

The Embrace

"Dogs sometimes are injured during these races, and sometimes die, but there is certainly risk in any kind of athletic endeavor."

—West Virginia State Senator Bill Ihlenfeld

In the years which followed the passage of Amendment 13, the walls began to close in on the final remnants of greyhound racing in the United States. In April of 2020, the Birmingham Racecourse announced the permanent closure of its track, ending greyhound racing in Alabama. Like Mobile Greyhound Park and VictoryLand, it could not survive without the kind of expanded gambling that the state's conservative legislature would seemingly never approve. Two months later, Gulf Greyhound Park also announced it was shuttering, taking the Lone Star state off the racing map as well.

Meanwhile, we were approached for the first time by the dogmen themselves, through lawyer Jerry Crawford. Our first true contact with him occurred in early 2019, when we discovered that greyhounds were being sold and shipped to China, where an illegal racing subculture was now evident. Carey took the story to the *Des Moines Register*, pointing out that one of the dogs that had been shipped to China was a former track champion at Iowa Greyhound Park in Dubuque. Even before the *Register* story was published, Crawford requested a meeting and offered up a draft industry policy to prohibit Chinese exports. The policy was only voluntary and had no real enforcement mechanism.

Although we had not directly spoken to Crawford before, we knew he was a formidable foe. Christine had argued against him (and lost) at a meeting of the Iowa Racing and Gaming Commission years beforehand. But now, on a bigger stage, Jerry was not necessarily in the catbird seat. He innately understood the mechanisms of power and clearly saw the reputational danger presented by the export of American racing dogs to China. Christine offered language to strengthen his proposed new industry policy, knowing that this policy was more a public relations tool than anything else.

A few months later, we heard from Crawford again. He said he now represented some Arkansas kennel owners who wanted to discuss a possible wind down of racing. We replied that we would happily meet, but only in person and in Boston. Carey wanted to make sure that any negotiation occurred on our home court, right beneath the Wonderland sign in our office. Crawford agreed and flew to Boston, where he met Carey, Christine, and Wayne Pacelle. Wayne and Jerry had known each other for years and worked together on unrelated animal welfare issues. The four of us talked for hours, and Crawford was given a preview of the endgame plan that was about to unfold. We were readying the strongest push ever to end greyhound racing in its final states, coupled with a federal bill to outlaw gambling on dog racing nationwide.

Crawford expressed sympathy for those who still worked in the industry, while also conceding that he agreed with some of our animal welfare concerns. On more than one occasion, he pointed out that these were generational businesses, and described how difficult it was for the dogmen to let go of a way of life that had been passed down through families. According to Crawford, some of the last industry holdouts were ready for a transition but demanded a phase-out period of more than a decade. This was impossible for us to even consider. After all, every extra year meant that more dogs would suffer and die.

In early August, Jerry Crawford offered us an eight-year phase-out period for greyhound racing in Arkansas, with an additional two years of subsidy payments being directed to a transition fund for industry workers. He framed this as something he didn't think the industry would accept, but that he could convince them of in time. In effect, Jerry was attempting to make us negotiate against ourselves, and from a ridiculous starting point. After a lot of soul-searching, Christine responded in writing with a counterproposal that included a similar phase-out but added a year-to-year reduction of races as well as a requirement that Jerry's other clients in Iowa publicly announce that they, too, would end dog racing. Months passed without a response. Then, in October, the news broke that Southland would be terminating greyhound racing completely by the end of 2022. It turned out that the entire time Jerry had been "negotiating" with us, he had already been given an ultimatum by track owner Delaware North: accept a phase-out of racing by the end of 2022 or face the immediate shutdown of the only dog track in Arkansas.

The announcement that racing would soon be suspended at Southland was a gigantic victory. The writing was on the wall for the American industry! Weeks later, Iowa Greyhound Park in Dubuque indeed announced that it would wind down and cease racing in 2022 as well. This left West Virginia as the final holdout. Tri-State and Wheeling Island would be the last American tracks left standing, and the American industry was now hanging by the slimmest of threads, clinging to its final lifeline: the $17 million in annual subsidies propping up racing in the Mountain State.

In early 2020, West Virginia Senate President Mitch Carmichael filed a bill to end these subsidies. We worked overtime, preparing for battle, and were hopeful that Carmichael would follow in the footsteps of Florida's Tom Lee to become the champion the greyhounds needed. We pulled out the stops and used many of the successful techniques that had proven effective during the Amendment 13 drive. This time, our audience would not be millions of voters, but the 134 legislators sitting in Charleston. We published an informational website called "greyhoundracingfacts. org," retained four excellent lobbyists, aired thousands of dollars in radio ads, released a string of targeted web ads, and launched a massive grassroots push.

The greyhound breeders countered with a disciplined lobbying effort that was led by Wheeling area Senators Ryan Weld and Bill Ihlenfeld. Both lawmakers were former prosecutors and made a disingenuous, but compelling, case that dog racing should continue. First, they denied the subsidies for greyhound racing were in fact "subsidies." This helped distract attention away from the merits of propping up a dying industry. It also gave them a platform to attack the facts by shooting the messengers, including President Carmichael himself.

On the floor of the Senate, Weld and Ihlenfeld took their deception to yet another level. Anti-racing advocates were blasted for not offering an adoption plan. This talking point relied on the fact that most lawmakers lacked knowledge about the culture of dog racing and did not understand that the kennels alone controlled the fate of greyhounds. The two lawmakers also hypocritically capitalized on an overwhelming dislike of outsiders—even though they themselves were relying on a dogman from Massachusetts as their spokesperson! Steve Sarras was the President of the West Virginia Kennel Owners Association but actually hailed from George Carney's Brockton, Massachusetts. In fact, he had raced dogs at the old Raynham Park until our 2008 ballot question forced him out.

State Senator Bill Ihlenfeld, February 29, 2020
(WV Legislative Photography/Will Price)

Senator Ihlenfeld vouched for dog racing, reasoning "there aren't many industries in our state that we control, that is ours alone, and we're close to being the only game in town when it comes to this industry." He told his colleagues that "instead of kicking this to the curb, we ought to embrace it." Ihlenfeld cynically rationalized greyhound injuries and deaths. "Dogs sometimes are injured during these races, and sometimes die," he told his Senate colleagues, "but there is certainly risk in any kind of athletic endeavor."

Despite a valiant effort by Senator Carmichael and our entire team, the bill to defund greyhound racing was defeated in the Senate by an agonizing margin of 11 to 23. We lost every Senate Democrat, and only split the Republican caucus. Even though he did not succeed, Mitch Carmichael will forever share a bond with people he will likely never meet, a diverse group that includes Senator Pat Jehlen and Representative Carl Sciortino of Massachusetts, Senator Sheila Roberge and Representative Steve Vaillancourt of New Hampshire, lobbyist Michael Preston Green and greyhound advocate Caryn Wood of Arizona, advisor Marc Reichelderfer and Representative Carlos Guillermo Smith of Florida, and so many more.

Our greatest teacher has often been bitter defeat, which has provided invaluable insight for the next campaigns. This was certainly the case in West Virginia, as a bold wave of advocacy was about to emerge. In 2019, Christine had drafted a federal bill to outlaw dog racing and in late 2020, Congressman Tony Cárdenas of California came forward to champion it. In only a few short months, it earned the support of 16 legislative cosponsors. It was refiled in the 117th Congress, and by the Spring of 2022, had 100 congressional co-sponsors and endorsements from hundreds of animal protection groups, local animal shelters, anti-gambling organizations, international NGOs, and even rabbit rescues. Sadly, certain humane organizations refused to publicly support the US Greyhound Protection Act. When the greyhounds needed them the most, the Humane Society of the United States and the Humane Society Legislative Fund, the ASPCA, and the Animal League Defense Fund were nowhere to be found. It was 2000 all over again

These groups had chosen to distance themselves from the greyhound campaign because Wayne Pacelle and his new group, Animal Wellness Action, endorsed our federal bill first. Meanwhile, Wayne offered to use his many contacts to reach out directly to Lou Jacobs, who had controlled Delaware North operations for generations. Wayne let us know that the family's goal was to end greyhound racing at the last two West Virginia tracks within a few years. Most importantly, the company also pledged in writing to be neutral on our federal bill. By the Summer of 2022, greyhound racing only existed in two states and was on the verge of ending in Arkansas, truly leaving West Virginia as the last stand. The final two dog tracks, Tri-State and Wheeling Island, were the subject of scrutiny from every direction. The federal Greyhound Protection Act was slowly gathering support with each passing month.

Dog racing was now so isolated that it depended on simulcast bets that were being made remotely, at off-track betting parlors and over the internet. As we reached the endgame stage of the American greyhound debate, we started to focus on passing laws to outlaw this kind of wagering as well. In 2022, Kansas lawmakers adopted a greyhound simulcasting ban. In May of the same year, Oregon lawmakers passed a new law to restrict internet betting on greyhound racing. This was a major blow as racetracks nationwide use the Beaver State as a processing hub for pari-mutuel bets. Senate bill 1504, passed by legendary Senator Peter Courtney just before his retirement as the longest serving lawmaker in Oregon history, also made Oregon the 42nd state to outlaw live dog racing. On the floor, he lamented the sad fact that West Virginia, where he had attended high school, would be the final holdout for greyhound racing. "I think if I were in that legislature, I'd probably have something to say about that," Courtney told his colleagues in his final speech. "That saddens me because I am very fond of the state and her people."

These victories brought us to the very precipice of the mountain we had been slowly ascending for two decades. Our destination, the end of greyhound racing in the United States, was now in full view and appeared to be imminent. However, our strange odyssey was not yet complete. Our path held at least two more surprises, and a reminder that sometimes, when you think you are near the end of the journey, you find yourself back at the beginning.

CHAPTER 15

THE SECRET

> "Part of why I've come forward right now, is a guilty conscience for some of the things I've done and witnessed without putting up more of a fight."
>
> —Confidential Informant

In August of 2019, Carey received an unexpected message from someone within the industry. "Ben" had learned about greyhound racing through a romantic relationship with a lifelong greyhound breeder and trainer. He was offered a job with her family, and it wasn't long before he was asked to do things that felt wrong. Ben told himself it was just a part of the job, and he needed to find a way to fit in. This was an environment where animal cruelty and neglect were normal, just part of doing business. He heard coworkers discuss the way they used drugs to fix races, and saw slow dogs get shot and buried in mass graves. "I worked in the greyhound industry for thirteen years," Ben said. "I have a lot of info on the inside workings of this industry and specifically the nightmare death sentence of most dogs."

Ben also claimed that virtually all young greyhounds are still live lure trained, given small rabbits to tear apart. "I know that live jacks are still used by a lot of kennels . . . I have a lot of info I'd like to get off my chest and I think it will help you put an end to his horrible sport." As Carey listened to this mournful account, it became clear that Ben was struggling to make peace with the gruesome things he had seen—and in some cases, done—to these gentle dogs.

This wasn't the first time an industry insider had told us that live lure training was still happening. In 2010, we had been approached by longtime greyhound trainer Harry Marshall Rae. A generational dogman, Marshall had spent his entire life in the racing industry. He contacted us with an emotional story about how he could no longer live with all of the terrible things he had done to greyhounds, and expressed a desire to be absolved of his sins. Rae said he had personally witnessed live lure training, and claimed to have direct knowledge of greyhound death pits. Skeptical of his account, we kept records of his every phone call. Then one day, the old dogman managed to film live lure training in Texas by carrying around a soda can with a small camera hidden inside. Learning this, Carey put him in contact with the Iowa Racing and Gaming Commission, which opened an investigation and set up consultations with state police agencies in several states. Immediately following a meeting with law enforcement officials in Kansas, Rae received a phone call from his brother, who demanded that he shut up now—or else.

Meanwhile, Carey learned that Rae was playing multiple hands. He had also offered his footage to the owners of Bluffs Run in Iowa, in exchange for a no-show job and a brand-new truck. Carey was furious, and immediately cut off contact. A year later, the news broke that a Texas greyhound breeder had lost his state license and was facing criminal charges for live lure training. The key witness was none other than Marshall Rae, and the sanctions were based on footage he had taken. Against his better judgment, Carey made contact with Rae again, and offered to help him tell his story to the media. The *New York Times* was interested, despite the obvious problems Rae presented as a source. The *Times* began to put a story together, and it briefly appeared that this decades-old dirty secret would finally come to light. More than thirty years had passed since Geraldo Rivera had first reported on live lure training, and clearly, the industry had never stopped this despicable practice.

Then everything fell apart. Upon arriving at work one morning, Carey came across messages posted on the internet by Rae, announcing to the entire world that he was about to tell his story to the *New York Times*. Carey picked up the phone and read him the riot act. Why was he trying to sabotage this incredible opportunity? As it turns out, Carey only knew a small part of the story. A few hours later, Rae was arrested by the Federal Bureau of Investigation and charged for his involvement in a plot to extort Earl Ray Tomblin, the Governor of West Virginia. Tomblin's family had been involved in greyhound racing for decades, and ran a well-known breeding kennel. Not a very clever crook, Rae used an official state website contact form to threaten the Governor with exposure unless a particular Boy Scout troop of his choice received $50,000. When Rae went to prison, greyhound breeders fantasized that Carey would be charged in the conspiracy as well. What they did not understand was that he was a witness, not a target. Their attempt to smear him for trying to expose their own cruel practices showed just how clueless the industry was.

In the intervening years, we continued to receive intelligence that live lure training was indeed an ongoing standard practice. It was the "open secret" of an industry that would rather risk exposure than change its ways. On several occasions, we hired investigators to follow up on leads, with no success.

But things felt differently with our anonymous informant, "Ben." He not only claimed to have trained with live lures himself, but told us where his racing kennel had done the deed, the methods that were used, and names of other kennel operators he had seen commit the cruel act. We were even able to independently verify many of the key assertions. Everything was apparently happening at a remote property in Keota, Oklahoma, an area notorious for other forms of animal cruelty, including cockfighting.

Sensing a rare opportunity, Carey reached out to Pete Paxton, an accomplished animal cruelty investigator. Pete was a quintessential chameleon, outwardly unremarkable in virtually every way. Yet beneath his average appearance burned a passion to stop cruelty, even if he had to witness it firsthand. He had recently published a book about his successful exposé of puppy mills and agreed to take our case, although he was doubtful live lure training could be happening on any real scale. We gave him all of our case files, including the most recent allegations from Ben.

Live lure training in Keota, Oklahoma, March 3, 2020 (GREY2K USA Worldwide)

On March 3, 2020, Pete filmed greyhound live lure training for the first time. The footage was genuinely evil. Three people, including prominent greyhound breeder Wesley Parvin, were caught live-baiting dozens of greyhounds with helpless rabbits at a coursing field in Keota. Young dogs were brought out in groups and placed in starting boxes. Live rabbits were then carried out, dangled by their back legs in front of the dogs, and let loose. The dogs would chase the rabbits, pin them to the ground, and tear them limb from limb. After the rabbit stopped moving or refused to flee, the men would retrieve the body and tie it to a rope, waving the bleeding and screaming animal to entice the dogs one last time. This process of torture and death was repeated over and over again, for hours. What we saw was utterly depraved, one of the worst things Pete had ever seen in all his years as an undercover animal cruelty investigator.

The next day, Pete filmed live lure training again in Keota, this time by local Deputy Sheriff Jason Martin and his teenage daughter, ironically named "Brooklyn." Before starting, Martin took out a shotgun, slowly scanning the surrounding fields. This was a reminder to Pete of the real danger he found himself in. But, of course, this only made him more determined.

We compiled a detailed report on Martin and Parvin, which included the footage Pete obtained and a frame-by-frame description and dossier of all of the perpetrators he had caught on tape. Christine then wrote to the US Attorney for the Eastern District of Oklahoma and to the Haskell County District Attorney, asking them to enforce state animal protection laws. She also reminded them of a new federal anti-cruelty law called the Preventing Animal Cruelty and Torture Act, which made it a felony to engage in "conduct in which one or more living non-human mammals, birds, reptiles, or amphibian is purposely crushed, burned, drowned, suffocated, impaled, or otherwise subjected to serious bodily injury." Violators faced fines and imprisonment of up to seven years.

Two months later, Pete documented live lure training in Elgin, Texas, at the farm of greyhound breeder Tori Shepherd. Born in 1937, James Doyle Shepherd had worked for decades as a truck driver before retiring to raise greyhounds full time. He achieved industry prominence in 2010, when one of his "U Too" litters was the top winning litter at the annual NGA Meet. In 2014, James passed away at the age of 76, leaving the farm to his wife Ila. When she passed away in 2019, the family greyhound business was left to their granddaughter, Tori. Within a few years, Tori was breeding a large number of dogs. Many notable greyhound owners had recently purchased dogs raised by Tori, including NGA Board member Jay Childs, who lived only a few miles away from the Shepherd farm.

When Pete first checked out the Shepherd operation, he quickly confirmed that rabbits were kept on the property. The makeshift training track also contained a small, enclosed area, where baby pigs were held. This was extremely suspicious, but Pete did not document anything conclusive on that first visit. The case broke open when Tori posted a video on Facebook, which depicted herself and an accomplice encouraging pit bulls to maul two baby pigs. When we saw this footage, Pete immediately returned to Texas. On the very first day, he filmed live lure training of greyhounds. The cruel conduct was filmed at the Shepherd farm a second time two days later. We compiled the evidence and provided it to Texas authorities.

Meanwhile, Iowa Greyhound Association lawyer Jerry Crawford caught wind of our investigation, and took a particular interest in the Elgin case. Two IGA Board members were among those who had purchased dogs from Shepherd and were now racing them in Iowa and other states. As if we were friends and partners, Jerry got word to us that he was "disappointed" we had not approached him with our information first. Once more, he wanted to make a scandal involving his clients go away.

By the middle of July, the investigation was on the verge of making headlines. Knowing we were running out of time, Pete wanted to take one last shot at filming live lure training at a third farm. Logic would suggest this would be nearly impossible, since by this time, every greyhound breeder in the country must have known that we had footage from Oklahoma and Texas. But we followed Pete's intuition, and were rewarded. On July 16, he filmed live lure training at yet another property, this time at a greyhound farm that was only two miles away from the NGA headquarters in Abilene, Kansas.

The live lure trainer in Abilene was none other than Ursula O'Donnell, who had been arrested in 2002 as an accomplice to Robert Rhodes in a conspiracy to kill thousands of unwanted greyhounds by shooting them in the head for a $10 fee. Ursula had been a fugitive from justice, and felony animal cruelty charges against her were only dropped when Rhodes died before trial. In the years since, Ursula had been repeatedly reprimanded and fined by state regulators, including cases in which dogs in her control had tested positive for banned drugs. Despite this checkered past, the NGA had taken zero action against her. When the NGA was asked by a *Florida New Times* reporter in 2010 why it hadn't sanctioned Ursula, a spokesman falsely asserted that "there have been no negative incidents involving Ms. O'Donnell since that time, and her ability to be licensed by racing states remains intact." Here was another reminder of the closing of ranks within the greyhound industry. Even bad apples were welcomed in this tight, insular world. So much for "policing themselves."

On a hot summer morning, Pete filmed Ursula as she pulled onto a coursing field with a load of greyhounds and nonchalantly set jackrabbits loose to be torn apart. She watched casually, almost with a bored expression, as the helpless animals screamed for their lives. Was she truly so jaded that torturing animals was just "another day at the office?" We submitted the results of the Kansas investigation to state and federal law enforcement agencies, and shared all three investigations with racing regulators in Iowa, Florida, Texas, and Arkansas. More than one hundred greyhounds linked to these live racing facilities were racing in North America, including dozens of dogs in key racing states. Forty-two years after the initial *20/20* exposé, we had finally proven that this cruelty was as much a part of the racing industry as it had ever been. What's more, greyhound breeders had not only continued to torture small animals, but had been lying to the public about it for years.

On July 26, 2020, the three investigations were reported by longtime investigative journalist Jim Defede of *CBS* in Miami. As expected, he was met with forceful denials from the industry folks he interviewed, none of whom realized we had them on tape. Wesley Parvin and Ursula O'Donnell each lost their state racing licenses, but sadly they never faced any criminal charges.

True to form, the National Greyhound Association ignored the live lure cases altogether. For decades, it had claimed that the use of live bait was not acceptable, and that violators would be held accountable. But when key members were caught red-handed, the NGA was noticeably silent. The only industry affiliated voice who spoke out was Rory Goree, who had, at this point, become an open critic of greyhound racing and a voice of conscience. "It is difficult not to wonder who knew the secrets or why this practice continues," Rory wrote in a blog post. "Could 'it's against the rules' and 'we will kick anyone out caught doing so' just be pat responses to keep the public at bay? Perhaps the NGA has buried its head in the sand."

During these later years, Rory Goree had realized that he had been misled by his friends in the dog racing world. He had recently begun speaking out for horses and was ultimately removed from the Arizona Racing Commission because of this advocacy. Over time, he and Carey had become allies, proof that change is always possible.

A year later, in June of 2021, Pete filmed greyhound live lure training for a fourth time, at the Colorado farm of John and Jill Lashmet. The Lashmets ran one of the largest greyhound breeding operations in the industry, and had owned the 2019 national win leader, named LK's Crush N It. When questioned by local law enforcement and state investigators, John bragged about his thirty years in the business and described in knowing detail how "jacking" works. He recounted that he had started out as a young boy in Kansas helping to round up and bludgeon hundreds of rabbits at a time. To Lashmet, "damn jackrabbits" were just "rodents" and could be killed at any time (and in any way, apparently). Despite the 67-year-old's recorded admissions, the Weld County Sheriff's Office took no action and tried to hide the body cam footage of officers' neighborly visit to Lashmet. Deputies closed the case as quickly as possible, disingenuously citing a "lack of evidence."

Then, like the proverbial "man on a white horse," an investigator with the state's Division of Racing took up the case. Anthony Milne visited Lashmet, questioned him, and warned him to stop all illegal activity. He let Lashmet know that he would be keeping an eye on him. Lashmet immediately confessed that he had in fact been live lure training, and when his admission reached track owner Delaware North, his dogs were banned from all American tracks. Of course, we wanted to see punishment, but the thought that one of the cruelest greyhound breeders in the country might be out of the rabbit killing business provided utmost satisfaction.

Colorado greyhound breeder John Lashmet, June 10, 2021
(Weld County Sheriff's Office)

It seemed as though the industry's secrets were finally coming out. As the live lure cases broke, another longtime problem within the dog racing industry was revealed with the federal indictment of kennel operator Jon Stidham of Iowa in January 2022. Stidham operated Kennel Supply, LLC and distributed more than fifty types of drugs to breeding farms across the country. Among other counts, he pleaded guilty to illegally selling the anabolic steroid methyltestosterone to greyhound trainers. He regularly distributed B12 injectables to perk up slower greyhounds and even created "DIY vet kits" with skin staplers and tape so that his fellow greyhound breeders could mend dogs on the cheap. Stidham also sold the needles and ink to tattoo young pups with racing numbers, as well as the crude whips found in racing kennels nationwide. This wasn't the first time Stidham was named in a racing scandal, either. In 2015, nine of his own greyhounds had tested positive for the artificial growth hormone ractopamine. On July 29, 2022, he was ordered to spend 15 months in prison, pay a fine of $7,500, and forfeit $527,510 in proceeds from illegal drug sales.

Carey had sounded the alarm about Stidham seven years before, emphasizing that as the President of the Iowa Greyhound Association, he would have access to a built-in clientele. In 2016, we had filed an official complaint and then followed with our report, *No Confidence: Drugs in the American Greyhound Racing Industry.* But it was not until a West Virginia animal hospital also raised concerns that the Department of Justice finally took action. In a raid of Stidham's property, federal authorities found and seized over 4,000 capsules of methyltestosterone, doctored prescription forms, a list of dog names, falsified business records, and over $51,000 in cash.

After so many years of greyhound suffering, it appeared that the dogmen were finally being exposed. The news revelations were concrete proof that as long as tracks exist, and people continue to breed dogs for the gambling industry, there would be an endless flow of cruelty and corruption. We were heartened to see key members of the racing world face justice from time to time, but it was not enough to unearth them one-by-one, farm-by-farm. Greyhound racing had to end completely.

During the many years we fought to help greyhounds, we were always deeply motivated by the mission and felt grateful for the opportunity to do this work. The real reward, though, ended up being the rescue of a single dog. That dog was Brooklyn.

Chapter 16

The Homecoming

"Everything I know I learned from dogs."

—Nora Roberts

A few days after Florida voters outlawed greyhound racing in November 2018, Carey and Christine received a series of photos of Brooklyn at the Canidrome. Taken by volunteer Robin Reich, they depicted a haggard dog who had spent a lifetime alone in a barren cell. No longer facing the threat of being killed at the track, he was still waiting to be rescued. On New Year's Eve, he was shipped across the world for the final time, to the National Greyhound Adoption Program in Pennsylvania. Caryn Wood, who had agreed to manage the flights of all dogs coming into the US, waited anxiously for the news of his safe arrival. Like Christine, she was fearful that he would not survive the trip. In Macau, newspapers heralded his departure, chronicling every step of his journey. Thankfully, he arrived safely in Philadelphia, though he was underweight, his coat dull and dirty, and had large sores visible on his legs. Thirteen teeth, worn down to the roots after years of chewing on the bars of his cage, were removed. David Wolf, Bobbie Gunning, and the NGAP team kept him for weeks, trying to restore his health.

When Christine first saw Brooklyn, she threw her arms around the thin dog. She still couldn't believe he was alive. She even checked his ear tattoos to be absolutely sure that this was the same dog that had been photographed at the Canidrome in 2011! His fur was so soft, his eyes so big and deep. He had something indescribably gentle and wise about his whole being. For years, she had had a dreamlike vision of a white dog with brown spots, and here he was! She whispered in his ear that he was finally coming home, then dashed out of the shelter with Carey like there was no tomorrow. Our friends Deno and Jeorge Seder were there and recorded it. Who knew how long Brooklyn could survive? Days, weeks, or months— but certainly no more than that.

Albano Martins and team say goodbye to Brooklyn, January 8, 2019
(Albano Martins/ANIMA Macau)

Over the next few days, Brooklyn was confused about his newfound freedom. He wandered from room to room, unsure of what he was supposed to do next. He happily co-existed with Gina, a fawn greyhound Carey and Christine had rescued from Florida's Derby Lane, but was less excited about the four cats awaiting him in Massachusetts. He made fast friends with everyone at the GREY2K USA Worldwide office, especially our assistant Caroline Williams. She loved to walk him and would spend time with him each day, giving him lots of treats. She also learned how to therapeutically massage his frail body. Caroline was Team Brooklyn all the way.

Brooklyn had a mischievous side, too. At home, if Carey or Christine turned their backs for even a moment, he would scramble up their narrow wooden stairs in search of the cats. He managed to steal sips of coffee and sambuca right off the table and ate everything in sight. Our new boy was quite the fun-loving hound.

These happy days lasted for just five short weeks, until Brooklyn started to limp. He hesitated to put weight on his left front leg, exhibiting the lameness every greyhound adopter truly dreads. He seemed uncomfortable and would sometimes cry while sitting on the couch. Carey and Christine hoped it was a torn muscle, but he did not respond to pain medication at all. The situation deteriorated rapidly, and a visit to the Concord Animal Hospital confirmed the worst: Brooklyn had bone cancer. A violent tumor had already eaten through his left shoulder, and the leg could completely collapse at any moment. Everyone was devastated including Dr. Stephen Wilson, the veterinarian who made the diagnosis. After delivering the tragic news, he followed Brooklyn out to the car, not wanting to let him out of his sight. After everything Brooklyn had endured, how could this sweet dog lose his life only weeks after finding a family?

We were faced with a grim decision, to say goodbye to Brooklyn or help him fight. The standard course of treatment involved amputation of the leg, followed by chemotherapy. Was Brooklyn capable of making this adjustment, after everything he had been through? Was it fair to him? What would he want, if he could understand the situation? These questions hung in the air, painful reminders of all the dogs that had died in Macau. The next day, Brooklyn was seen by a kind veterinary surgeon, who recommended immediate surgery and warned us of his delicate condition. Carey and Christine hardly slept that night, terrified but vigilant in making sure Brooklyn remained completely immobile. We brought him to the hospital in the early morning, then anxiously waited. The call finally came, and the news was mercifully good. In fact, just as the surgeon started to remove the cancerous leg, it had shattered in her hands. We had made the right decision, and just in time to save him from a traumatic end.

In the weeks that followed, Brooklyn gained strength and learned to live as a tripod. He received chemotherapy treatments, and was accepted into a trial for a new treatment protocol. This trial was a godsend, but prompted another scare when Brooklyn had to be hospitalized due to an adverse reaction midway through. On the morning after this close call, our staff members each took turns sitting with the tired dog, slowly caressing his face. We all realized how delicate he was, and that each day was a gift.

Despite these challenges, Brooklyn remained upbeat in recovery. He endeared himself to Gina, who woke up one night, walked over to his bed, and laid down next to him. She had never shared a bed with another dog! The two learned to play together despite Brooklyn's physical limitation, chasing each other around the room while galloping and throwing toys in the air. Although most of the cats now preferred to stay upstairs, our black shorthair Little Ricky loved to come down and visit. Each evening, he ventured down the stairs in the dark of night after everyone had gone to sleep, where he would sit and stare, wide-eyed with amazement, at the sleeping dog that had come from China. For his part, Brooklyn's favorite time of day was his return home from the office. When we opened the front door, he would burst inside, hoping to find a cat waiting in the foyer.

In August, Brooklyn went to the beach for the first time. He made his way across the sand and stopped at the water's edge, gazing in wonder at the crashing of the frothy waves. A young boy approached, and asked Carey what had happened to his leg. Carey replied that Brooklyn was a cancer survivor, and that this was his first time seeing the ocean. The child ran away, but returned a few minutes later. He held out his hand, which contained some loose change he had found in the sand, and shyly said he wanted us to have it to help Brooklyn. Touched, Christine reached into her beach bag and gave the boy her blue "Save the Greyhounds" wristband, which he put on with delight.

Brooklyn at home on the couch, Arlington, Massachusetts, August 6, 2019
(Carey M. Theil)

Summer came and went. Before long, the leaves were falling, and a canvass of gold, orange, and red foreshadowed the bitter cold that would soon arrive. Brooklyn continued to go to the office each day, starting off each morning by waiting on the first floor of the building to greet our fellow tenants as they arrived for work. Whenever a new face appeared, he would rush up in a flurry of big tail wags. The objects of his affection always smiled broadly and laughed as they stroked his long face and cradled his velvety ears. How could this dog still be so full of love and serenity, after enduring a lifetime of loneliness and despair, and now losing a leg? It seemed that no matter what happened to him, he held no grudges and lived each day to the fullest. His attitude of complete forgiveness is something that we have tried to emulate to this day.

As Brooklyn settled into this new life, change was in the air. Albano Martins and Christine led a global rescue program to airlift all of the Canidrome dogs to safety. Many of the 532 survivors were transported to groups in the United States under the guidance of Caryn Wood. She obtained all the necessary paperwork for each dog, assigned them to groups, arranged the flights, and got very little sleep for almost a year due to the time difference between Arizona and Macau. NGAP of Philadelphia accepted over 100 greyhounds into its program while other, smaller rescue groups found room for ten or twenty at a time. Stefania Traini and Massimo Greco of Pet Levrieri led the European adoption program and also directed dogs to individual groups in the United Kingdom and Ireland. It was a Herculean effort, and one that taught Christine that no matter the difficulties, the distance, or the expense, greyhound advocates can join together to bring dogs to safety. Clever Albano had forced the track owner to pay for the flights, so all the money that Christine had raised was used directly to sponsor arriving dogs. As with the 2016 Tucson adoption program, she offered $500 per dog to all groups willing to accept Canidrome greyhounds into their networks. One of the most surprising things we learned was that the Macau dogs were far healthier than we had expected. Few groups reported severe medical issues, and in particular, the specter of osteosarcoma did not often rear its head. This was a silver lining for the surviving Canidrome dogs.

Then, two weeks after the world was shut down by the COVID-19 pandemic, we almost lost Brooklyn again. He had come into the office with Christine and was particularly energetic that day. He began running about in circles and chasing Gina all around the conference room table. This went on for some time. Then, breathless, he suddenly collapsed on his bed and would not get up. He laid down on his side, immobile. Alarmed, Christine called Dr. Wilson, who believed that Brooklyn may have had a stroke. On his advice, we rushed Brooklyn to specialists at the Massachusetts Veterinary Referral Hospital, where the initial prognosis was grim. Although doctors held out some hope that he might recover, their best guess was that cancer had spread to his brain and the situation was terminal. For the next few days, Brooklyn underwent a series of tests and neurological examinations. Could our intrepid dog, who had been shipped from Australia to Macau as a puppy, lived his adult years in a concrete cell at the Canidrome, survived a leg amputation, and finally found stability, now have reached his end?

The dreaded phone call from Brooklyn's doctor finally came. But to our relief and amazement, Brooklyn was cancer-free! We rejoiced and could barely contain ourselves. The doctor let us know that our handsome hound had suffered a spinal stroke, or fibrocartilaginous embolism (FCE). This is a neurological disorder from which most dogs recover. It seemed as though Brooklyn's luck had held. And they say only cats have nine lives! We rushed back to the hospital to pick him up.

Unfortunately, our relief faded when we realized how delicate he still was. Brooklyn was carried back to our car by hospital attendants, just as he had been carried inside for treatment days before. He was still unable to stand, which meant he was incapable of going outside to relieve himself. He had no appetite, and appeared to be in a state of depression. For weeks, we never left his side, knowing that we could lose him at any time. He cried and moaned unless someone rubbed and petted him continuously, something Christine learned to do while working on her laptop by day and (seemingly) while sleeping next to him at night. With each "accident," Carey would flip him over and Christine would wash a rotating series of orthopedic beds to keep him comfortable and dry.

As tiring as this routine was, we decided that if Brooklyn wouldn't give up, then neither would we. When he refused to eat, we obtained an appetite stimulant for him. Due to the pandemic, it was very difficult to obtain pee pads, but Christine put her New Jersey shopping skills to work and managed to buy two big boxes containing hundreds of disposable doggy pads. Then, on the advice of board member Charmaine Settle, she gave Brooklyn a dose of super-strength CBD oil. This turned out to be just what he needed! He took one dose and stood up on his own for the first time since his stroke. It was yet another miracle.

When we had picked him up at the hospital after the initial tests, Christine got a strong feeling that the attending staff expected to see us again very soon, assuming that caring for a severely disabled dog would be too much. They sent Brooklyn home with a little bit of pain reliever and nothing else. With no dispute, they would be ready to take him back and put him down whenever the time came. As we navigated this ordeal, we started to think about fundamental inequities in veterinary medicine. Even the word veterinarian, derived from the Latin term for "beasts of burden," consigns nonhuman animals like dogs, cats, and pigs to a lesser status. Brooklyn would receive only the care that we, the humans, agreed to pay for. He was at our mercy. For the first time, we contemplated the idea that veterinary care should be a fundamental right and considered how many loving animals are killed for lack of funds, or simply because people are not informed about the options available. So just as Carey had discovered the osteosarcoma trial that undoubtedly saved Brooklyn's life, he made a promise that he would do everything he could to advocate for this sweet dog in what was truly an imbalanced system.

Over the next six months, we did a number of things that made a big difference for Brooklyn. We contacted world renowned behaviorist Dr. Amy Marder, now practicing in a neighboring town. She had seen Brooklyn when we first adopted him, and put us in touch with an expert in canine rehabilitation, Dr. Suzy Starr of Paws in Motion in Natick. Dr. Starr, who truly lived up to her name, was willing to take on a new client and open up her clinic to us each week. She was compassionate, smart, and dedicated. She stretched Brooklyn, massaged him, and helped him heal. When Brooklyn was afraid of standing in the hydrotherapy booth, Dr. Starr had her husband build a special platform that allowed him to keep his front leg stable (and out of the water) while she supported his back legs.

After a few stressful months, Brooklyn began to recover, and every day with him became more precious than ever. He was more fragile now, like a delicate angel. Carey became his legs, carrying him outside to relieve himself several times a day. Brooklyn never regained his ability to walk in a coordinated way, but that did not stop him from bouncing around in the grass and crouching to smell the flowers of Christine's garden. The funny thing is that he was still very strong, and kicked like a horse in his sleep! He had bouts of anxiety, but he was largely happy and healthy.

Altogether, our time with Brooklyn lasted for more than three glorious years. Periodic veterinary checks were always negative for the return of cancer. In the MVRH oncology department, he became a symbol of hope to the families who were confronting the same terrible disease in their dogs. And so Brooklyn lived out his days with us, surrounded by friends and the many people who loved him. This was the greatest time in our lives, and we would happily have sustained it forever.

But alas, in the Spring of 2022 cancer did return. Brooklyn received additional chemotherapy treatments from Dr. Mitchell Kaye, and the three of us tried to decide what was best for Brooklyn. So much had been stolen from him, from the time he was a puppy. We tried to put Brooklyn's dignity and desires at the center of these final weeks. Christine did everything she could think of to get Brooklyn to eat even a little more each day. Carey held him up while he relieved himself, a task Brooklyn could no longer accomplish by himself. Gina rarely left his side, and Little Ricky laid next to him, purring, for hours. Even as the end approached, Brooklyn was happy to be with his family and wanted to stay.

In early June, we took Brooklyn to the beach one final time. Our dying dog happily floated in the ocean waves, while the bright sun washed across his white face. To our surprise and delight, the sea was unusually warm, especially for New England. It felt like a nice sauna, which was just what our dear boy needed. Christine and Gina watched as Carey cradled Brooklyn in the soothing flow.

For seven long days, Brooklyn barely clung to life, but he was too strong willed to leave. When he began to have trouble breathing, we knew the only choice was to aid his departure. And so we took Brooklyn to Dr. Wilson, who calmly gave our weak dog an injection to stop his heart. We told him we loved him and slowly stroked his rabbit-like fur as he gently passed away, his head resting on a soft pillow.

It was a breezy day, the second day of Summer, when we said goodbye to sweet Brooklyn. Afterwards, everything seemed like a dream. A beautiful force in our lives was simply gone. Gina was crushed. We knew we would never meet anyone like him again.

Epilogue

The Catalyst

"My heart aches but also rejoices for sweet Brooklyn."

—Eduardo A. Lopez

In the days following Brooklyn's death, thousands of grieving messages poured in from around the world. Animal advocates expressed a profound sadness for Brooklyn and for all the animals that have suffered at the hands of abusive industries. Supporters celebrated his life, referring to him as a hero, a legacy of hope, a gentle soldier, a catalyst for change, and a portrait of courage. Most of all, they just missed him, a dog they had never met but somehow loved with all their hearts. Remembrances were published by several news organizations and the *South China Morning Post* featured his story on the cover of its Sunday magazine, completing the circle that had started us on our journey with Brooklyn in 2011. *Fido Friendly*, *New York Lifestyles Magazine*, the *New Barker*, the *Sunday Tasmanian*, and *The Environmental Magazine* all published their own tributes. In Belgium, advocates held a private memorial service, walking through the woods with their rescued hounds. An acclaimed artist from California produced a pastel portrait of Brooklyn and an Australian songwriter recorded a song in his honor. Brooklyn's loss hung heavily over us, but the warm support we received made a huge difference.

Meanwhile, the movement Brooklyn helped inspire continued to march forward. Six days after his death, track owner Delaware

North publicly announced that, for the first time, it would support decoupling in West Virginia. In the months which followed, company representatives began quietly meeting with key lawmakers about a bill to end dog racing completely.

Brooklyn outside in the sun, May 11, 2021
(Maria Moyser/GREY2K USA Worldwide)

The fight to end greyhound racing was always an act of defiance, a call for compassion, and a demand that non-human animals be given due consideration in the political process. The battle itself was our teacher, as was gentle Brooklyn. He showed us that the most important thing is to love. The exploitation of greyhounds was a poison that threatened the integrity of everyone it reached, but resistance also drew out the better parts of who we are. Perhaps that is the real lesson—that only by facing darkness can we discover the light that exists in us all. This is something we discovered through the gentle eyes and happy smile of a speckled greyhound.

The history of greyhound racing is complicated, and the fight is far from over. For our part, which has spanned more than twenty years, it is a mosaic made up of a thousand small acts of heroism, moments of selfless bravery by volunteers, lawmakers, anti-gambling activists, and even members of the industry, who will forever be tied together by a shared purpose. Progress came in fits and starts, but in the end the dereliction of dog racing was outshined by the determination and grit of ordinary people trying to do what is right.

We believe that future generations will have a difficult time comprehending the twentieth century practice of using sensitive, loving dogs as numbers to gamble on. Why did it take so long to stop it? We cannot answer this question, but we hope that Brooklyn's story will spring forward into the hearts of all who read it and become a catalyst for positive change now and in the future.

AFTERWORD

SIMON PARRY

News stories come and go. What seems terribly important today is stale and irrelevant tomorrow. Issues that agitate and excite us one week can seem laughably trivial the next. As a freelance journalist who makes his living from one newspaper article to the next, I am painfully aware that stories that are the talk of the town today are often forgotten by tomorrow.

But some stories are different. Every now and then, a story comes along that strikes a chord with people and resonates deeply, moving them to action. Reporters call these rare events 'stories with legs' because they run and run. How apt, then, that a decade-old tale about the appalling plight of greyhounds at the Canidrome in Macau turned out to be such a story.

When I hopped onto a ferry from Hong Kong to Macau to investigate the issue for the South China Morning Post in 2011, I had no idea the controversy would ultimately have profound consequences—not only for the pitiful inhabitants of the Canidrome and the venue itself, but for the international animal welfare movement at large. After all, greyhound racing was nothing new. In the UK, the US, Australia, and Ireland, dogs lived and raced and died in roughly similar conditions. Certainly, the Canidrome was bleaker, more basic, and more brutal than its overseas counterparts, but it was fundamentally fulfilling the same unpleasant purpose: Racing magnificent animals to an early grave for entertainment and profit.

But there was a difference, and it lay in the starkness of the numbers. Unlike other countries, there was no way to adopt retired greyhounds in Macau. As soon as the dogs at the Canidrome were "finished" as racing dogs—usually when they had failed to be placed in three consecutive races—they were given a lethal injection and incinerated. They were put down at a rate of more than one a day, and of those, only a handful were euthanised because of racing injuries. Most were young and perfectly healthy dogs that had simply stopped winning. Meanwhile, younger replacement dogs were imported at an almost identical rate. No dog left the Canidrome alive. There was no chance of survival, and it was the sheer hopelessness of their situation that made it so unbearable.

There was no mention of Brooklyn in my original reports, and it wasn't my journalism that led to the ultimate closure of the Canidrome. The credit for that goes to Christine Dorchak and Carey Theil, and their colleagues at the GREY2K USA animal charity who read my article online and went to Macau to investigate—and ultimately save the lives of the remaining animals. Their haunting picture of a muzzled Brooklyn staring through the bars of his cage and their bold and tireless campaigning transformed a news story into an international issue and made possible a stay of execution for Brooklyn and the hundreds of greyhounds who were eventually adopted overseas after the Canidrome closed in 2018.

Brooklyn himself was the unlikeliest of heroes. As a racing dog, he was frankly hopeless. He failed to win a single race before or after his export from Australia, and would almost certainly have been euthanised within weeks if, by a quirk of fate, his sleek and intelligent features had not made him the poster boy for a global campaign. Some greyhounds may be born great, and some may achieve greatness—but Brooklyn was very definitely a dog who had greatness thrust upon him. And his fame came with a heavy price: Brooklyn was spared an immediate death sentence but spent eight years in his concrete cell at the Canidrome as the track's fate hung in the balance before seeing out the last three years of life cocooned with love in his adopted home in Massachusetts with Christine and Carey. How blissful and idyllic the final fifth of his life must have been compared with the horrors that preceded it.

However accidental his iconic status, there is no question Brooklyn's impact has been immense and far-reaching. The savagery of his situation and the long campaign to win his freedom has seen a shifting of attitudes towards greyhound racing worldwide and the real prospect of an end to a cruel so-called sport. Before Brooklyn, most people would shrug off greyhound racing as an unpalatable but generally harmless indulgence for gamblers. Now, growing numbers of people are shifting to activism and refusing to accept it in their states or to allow the lucrative canine exports that sustain the industry.

It isn't only the people who profit from the misery of greyhounds who feel the tide turning. The biggest event on Britain's horse racing calendar—the Grand National steeplechase, which has claimed the lives of 16 horses since 2000—was recently delayed and 118 people arrested when animal rights activists invaded the track. Brooklyn would no doubt have approved.

Our humanity and our moral progress are rightly judged by the way we treat our animals. Brooklyn's story forced people to question the morality of exploiting animals for profit without giving them so much as a sporting chance of survival. That is Brooklyn's legacy, and that is what makes him a true champion.

—Simon Parry, Journalist

(Albano Martins/ANIMA Macau)

ABOUT GREY2K USA

Formed in 2001, GREY2K USA Worldwide is the largest greyhound protection organization in the world. As a non-profit entity, it works to pass stronger greyhound protection laws and end the cruelty of dog racing on both national and international levels. It also promotes the rescue and adoption of greyhounds across the globe. For more information, go to GREY2KUSA.org.

ABOUT THE AUTHORS

CHRISTINE DORCHAK and CAREY THEIL are the co-founders of GREY2K USA Worldwide. As an attorney, Christine specializes in pari-mutuel law and has drafted laws to successfully prohibit dog racing in several states and countries. She has been featured in national publications including the Huffington Post, Forbes, and American Dog. A long-distance runner, she has competed in seven Boston Marathons. Carey has decades of legislative experience and has been quoted in hundreds of news articles about greyhound racing published across the globe. In his free time, Carey volunteers for various non-profit organizations and is a National Master in chess.

Poster by Cecie McCaffrey

About the Publisher

Lantern Publishing & Media was founded in 2020 to follow and expand on the legacy of Lantern Books—a publishing company started in 1999 on the principles of living with a greater depth and commitment to the preservation of the natural world. Like its predecessor, Lantern Publishing & Media produces books on animal advocacy, veganism, religion, social justice, humane education, psychology, family therapy, and recovery. Lantern is dedicated to printing in the United States on recycled paper and saving resources in our day-to-day operations. Our titles are also available as ebooks and audiobooks.

To catch up on Lantern's publishing program,
visit us at www.lanternpm.org

facebook.com/lanternpm
instagram.com/lanternpm
twitter.com/lanternpm